Chakras

GANESHA MANTRA

गजाननम् भूत गणादि सेवितम्

कपित्त्यजम्बू फल चारू भक्षणम्

उमा सुतम् शोक विनाशकारकम्

नमामि विघ्नेश्वर पाद पंकजम्

Chakras

by
Harish
Johari

Destiny Books
Rochester, Vermont

Destiny Books
One Park Street
Rochester, Vermont 05767

Library of Congress Cataloging-in-Publication Data

Johari, Harish, 1934–
Chakras: energy centers of transformation.

1. Chakras (Hinduism) 2. Kundalini. 3. Yoga. I. Title.
BL1215.C45J64   1987
294.5'4   87-15454
ISBN 0-89281-054-8 (pbk.)

Typography by Royal Type

Text design and production by Studio 31

Printed and bound in the United States

10 9 8

Destiny Books is a division of Inner Traditions International

Distributed to the book trade in Canada by Publishers Group West (PGW), Toronto, Ontario

Distributed to the book trade in the United Kingdom by Deep Books, London

Distributed to the book trade in Australia by Millennium Books, Newtown, N.S.W.

Distributed to the book trade in New Zealand by Tandem Press, Auckland

CONTENTS

Chakras

PREFACE

CHAKRAS ARE PSYCHIC CENTERS in the body that are active at all times, whether we are conscious of them or not. Energy moves through the chakras to produce different psychic states. Modern biological science explains this as the chemical changes produced by the endocrine glands, ductless glands whose secretions mix into the body's bloodstream directly and instantaneously. Ancient philosophers of the East related those changes with the five basic *tattva*s, or elements — earth, water, fire, air, and *akasha* (ether). These elements are constantly coming and going with the circadian rhythms inside the body. The ancient Indian science of Yoga therefore laid great emphasis on knowing these elements and on working accordingly, for the chakras are understood as the playground of the elements. In the ancient science of Svara Yoga (the yoga of conscious breathing), various methods to identify the presence of the tattva in the body are prescribed, and by mastering these techniques yogis can program themselves so as to accomplish much by using the least possible amount of energy. By the constant practice of *kshata chakra bhedana* (piercing the six chakras by visualization) and *mantra japa* (mantra recitation), they can finally transcend the tattvas, which dominate the five basic centers of the body — that is, the first five chakras — and thereby achieve the nondual consciousness that liberates them from the illusory world of *maya*.

Knowledge about the chakras can be a valuable key to introspection. It is possible to observe oneself and see energy moving through the various psychic centers. Religious practices such as fasting, charity, and selfless service cause the energy to flow into the higher centers; the dormant energy coiled in Muladhara ("root, base") Chakra becomes active — and begins its ascent. After the flow has reached the higher centers, the total attitude of the practitioner changes; this feeling is referred to repeatedly as a new birth. Maintaining the upward flow of energy then becomes the primary concern of such a person. The constant, simultaneous practice of visualization and mantra japa helps the aspirant to maintain the flow of energy in higher centers — and thus get beyond the tattvas.

Visualization requires proper images of the chakras. *Yantra*s, abstract forms or images of chakras drawn by visionary artists of the past, should be used. Such a tool without precepts is meaningless, however, and similarly, precepts without the proper tools offer no real growth. The illustrations in this book help the mind to retain the images of the chakras. Coloring the line drawings in a systematic way can further help in visualization, for one can repeat in the mind the sequence in which the color is painted, and thus mentally reconstruct the entire drawing. This will change the pattern of the brainwaves and the psychic makeup. To achieve the proper colors, one should consult the color illustrations that are provided. The following order should be used in coloring:

1. The petals of the chakra
2. The yantra of the chakra
3. The animal that carries the *bija* (seed, germ)
4. The bija sound
5. The Shakti of the chakra
6. The deity of the chakra

The same order should be used in visualization, that is, by mentally reconstructing the complete drawing of the chakra, one can develop the practice of abstract visualization, which in time will lead to deep meditation.

The line drawings should be colored to activate the right hemisphere of the brain; the introductory text should be studied to enrich the understanding and activate the left hemisphere. This will create a balance between the "thinker's brain" and the "artist's brain." Japa of the seed sounds (bija mantras) and following the law of *dharma* (righteousness, order) will assist the aspirant in achieving higher states of consciousness.

I would like to thank Mary Conors for preparing the line drawings for this book, based on paintings of the chakras that I had done earlier. I am very grateful to my teacher Shri C. Bal, who guided Isandeep Johari in preparing the colored illustrations, and to Heidi Rauhut for preparing the first copy of the revised text of the present edition. I also thank Elaine Minto for typing parts of the manuscript and helping me edit some of the chapters.

I am very thankful to H. H. Shripadji, Ganesh Baba, and Acharya Chandrashakhar Shastri for their clarification and guidance on various issues, and for enriching my knowledge by their teachings, blessings, and presence, which inspired me to undertake the job.

The teachings in this book come from my father, who practiced kshata chakra bhedana, and from different tantric scriptures, the writings of saints, and various scrolls that depict the chakras in a number of different ways. To assist in understanding the ancient concepts I have added many drawings and charts with the hope of enriching people's knowledge and helping them to comprehend the age-old Indian tradition of Tantra in a modern context.

Finally, I thank all of my friends and students whose valuable suggestions have helped me prepare this book, and hope that it in turn will be helpful as a guidebook to the chakras. Those who wish to study more about the planes mentioned in the different chakras are directed to my book *Leela** which is based on the "game" of knowledge. Additional aspects of the chakras are discussed in my book *Tools for Tantra.*†

Harish Johari
September 1987

363 Punjabpura
Bareilly, U.P.
India

---

* *Leela* London: Routledge & Kegan Paul, 1980).

† *Tools for Tantra* (Rochester, Vermont: Destiny Books, 1986).

CHAPTER ONE

Principles of Tantra

OF ALL EXISTING BODIES that express themselves through behavior, the human body is the most highly evolved. It is capable of self-expression and the realization of Truth beyond the realm of sensory perception. With the help of memory, imagination, and intuition, the human organism can understand and grasp laws inherent in nature, and can put those forces that are mysterious (if seen with an ordinary eye) to work for its benefit, growth, and development. With the perfect synchronization of interior and exterior rhythms, one can follow the path of least resistance and float freely in the ocean of the phenomenal world without getting drowned. To be precise, the human body is the most perfect instrument for the expression of consciousness.

Consciousness is the ultimate irreducible reality out of which, and by whose power, mind and matter proceed. The manifested reality as mind and matter is merely a fraction of the whole, or infinite reality. The mind limits consciousness so that the mind (the unit of consciousness) may have finite experiences. But in the broad spectrum from minerals to man there are various levels in which consciousness exists. In the world of names and forms (Sanskrit, *nama* and *rupa*) there is nothing absolutely conscious or absolutely unconscious. Consciousness and unconsciousness are harmoniously interwoven in the phenomenal world — and in man, consciousness exists as self-consciousness, which makes him different from all other forms of existing consciousness.

The chief centers of consciousness in human beings are found in the cerebrospinal system and in the upper brain. The cerebrospinal system is the first part of the organism to be developed after conception. From it the entire bodily form materializes. This system is a great generator of electrical energy and has a fantastic network of nerves that serve as connectors. The cerebrum, as it is called, keeps on producing electrical energy. Through fine nerves, this energy is constantly supplied to the organism, providing life force. At the back and

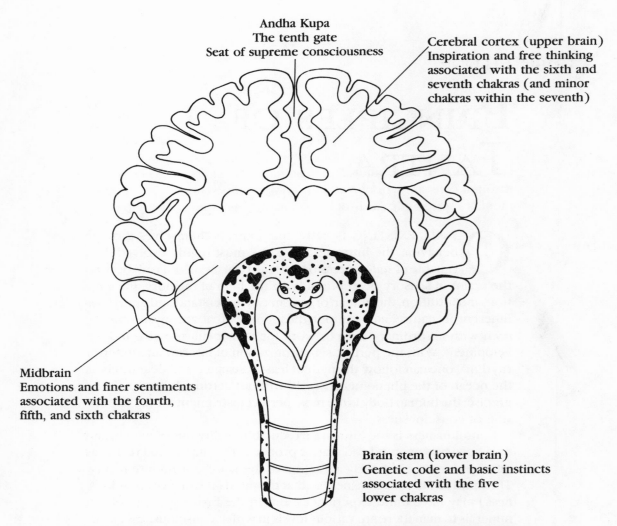

Andha Kupa
The tenth gate
Seat of supreme consciousness

Cerebral cortex (upper brain)
Inspiration and free thinking
associated with the sixth and
seventh chakras (and minor
chakras within the seventh)

Midbrain
Emotions and finer sentiments
associated with the fourth,
fifth, and sixth chakras

Brain stem (lower brain)
Genetic code and basic instincts
associated with the five
lower chakras

Diagram of the brain, its functions, and its relationship to the chakras.

at the base of the skull is the cerebellum — the mechanical brain, the organ of the subconscious mind. This is also known as the lower brain, the cobra brain, or the reptile brain. The upper brain is a comparatively later development as compared to the lower brain and it is more open to change.

The functioning of the entire human body is controlled by the cerebrospinal system, and the psychic centers are located in this system. For many centuries this knowledge has been handed down through the Hindu tantric tradition, which terms these psychic centers *chakras*. The belief is that in terms of balanced functioning, proper harmony should exist between the two brains — the upper brain (the organism of consciousness) and the lower brain (the seat of the subconscious mind). Modern studies of the upper and lower brains point toward inner conflict between the two and relate such conflict to behavioral patterns that are influenced and affected by it. These studies also point toward a basic dichotomy in human nature. This dichotomy is further substantiated by the presence of twin hemispheres of the brain, the cerebrum. We, as human beings, dwell in this duality and become victims of endless problems and complexes. To resolve this dichotomy, the most practical and plausible solution thus far applicable seems to be union between the upper and lower brain, and between its right and left hemispheres. Balanced union is achieved through constant work on all four components. Thus a basic requirement is a systematic study of human nature — a study of activities and functions of the human organism at work.

Many scientific investigations have been based on the study of dead or sick bodies from which living or healthy data is not revealed. Studies of the human organism in a wholistic manner have been made through the ancient sciences of Tantra and Yoga. Their results from research on healthy organisms have not yet been broadly correlated with the experimentations and explorations of Western medicine. Recently there has, of course, been a greater acceptance and broader application of exercise and breath control in post-operative and preventive measures, measures that have been translated directly from the tantric and yogic traditions and successfully adapted for the benefit of modern man. In order to attain a full understanding of humankind, the psychic dimensions — not simply the physical ones — must be examined thoroughly.

It is believed that the system through which transcendental union was first successfully sought is Yoga. The word yoga is derived from the Sanskrit root *yuj,* which means "to unite," "to join," "to add." If considered at the most profound level, this union is that between the individual consciousness and cosmic consciousness (that is, the soul with God). Yoga presents a practical method, a system that creates the state of unification of the two—the mental processes and the consciousness. Yoga is based on particular disciplines and exercises through which union may be obtained by anyone who chooses to adhere to the system prescribed by Yoga. According to that system, individual consciousness is a partial expression of cosmic consciousness, divine reality, the source, the substratum of the manifested universe. In essence, cosmic consciousness and individual consciousness are one, because both are consciousness and are indivisible. But the two are separated by sujectivity, and after the dissolution of this subjectivity, the "is-ness," or the individual consciousness, dissolves and union takes place. Realization of one's divine nature brings release from the trap of one's animal nature, which causes subjectivity and limited vision. In the language of Yoga this is called the "mind trap." In

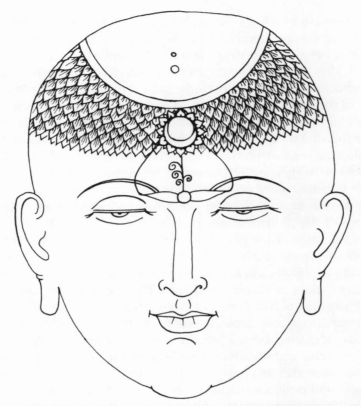

Yogic depiction of the important centers in the head

modern psychology the term *mind* is used in an entirely different context; there, it denotes the functional aspect of the brain that is responsible for thought, volition, and feelings. The brain is material reality and a tool of the mind, but the mind itself is not materially real. Modern scientists engage themselves in the search for nonmaterial reality in the material brain and its twin hemispheres. They search for the psyche. The core of ancient wisdom sheds much light on this subject and, if aptly researched and correlated, has much to offer in this field. In the realms of modern psychology and modern medical science this truth is understood to a certain extent. And to a degree, ancient knowledge is being researched and some scientists are pioneering correlations between this truth and their own observations.

In this day and age we are busy creating harmony between the rational approach and the emotional, or devotional, approach to the human psyche. The methods employed by the two systems — the modern and the ancient — have a basic difference in their approach. Yogis approach the psyche by searching for its cause in the mind and consciousness. Psychologists, on the other hand, seek to define it by studying behavior. The original yogic formula is to discover the self through self-research; the approach of scientists today is to observe others and not the Self, which is in everybody. Psychologists and other scientists involved with understanding consciousness study individuals and groups to determine the various dimensions of the mind. Yoga not only describes all mental states, aspects, and dimensions, but it advocates practical games to be played with the mind to control its functioning, to achieve peace, and to free it from the miseries and suffering caused by mental fluctuations and modifications. Inherent in Yoga are practical devices through which one may go beyond the mind's normal way of functioning.

Apart from its spiritual significance, the philosophy of Yoga has a moral value and is of much use in daily life. In yogic principles lies the foundation stone for better human relationships and collective peace. A basic yogic concept is stated in the maxim:

Sarve bhavantu sukhina
Sarve sant niramaya

May all be happy,
May all be in peace.

Principles established by yogic philosophy are universal and provide scope for overall development and advancement of all faculties of the mind. They provide the aspirant who works through Yoga the ability to stop at will all mental modifications. Constant practice of self-restraint helps the aspirant to become centered and quiet. It also quiets inner dialogue without effort. The fruit of yogic *sadhana* (practice) is the ability to rise above afflictions and to transcend the cognitive faculties, the perceptual world, and the attachment to the body and the senses. It provides the mind with habitual one-pointedness, undivided attention, perpetual peace, change in behavioral patterns and, finally, enlightenment.

One-pointedness is an attribute especially useful in this fast-paced, high-tech age. Peace within and around us, without distractions or disturbances, is essential to self-expression. Individually we need to understand our latent potential. We need self-research. We further need to understand ourselves as a microcosm, and to understand our relationship with the macrocosm. All physical sciences tend to divide man into many parts, whereas spiritual sciences perceive unity in diversity. Although it is indeed necessary to study part by part, it is also necessary to create a whole from those parts and to recognize one's own place in relation to that of others, who are similar parts. Too much individualism, subjectivity, and importance to one's own interests creates veils — and closes the windows of open-mindedness. An over-emphasis on the individual self will create feelings of loneliness and pessimism. Acknowledging this, the system of Yoga has identified five states of mind classification:

- Autism
- Stupefaction
- Restlessness
- One-pointedness
- Suppression

1. Autism (kshipta).

In this state one has neither the patience nor the intelligence necessary for contemplation of a supersensuous object and consequently cannot think of nor comprehend any subtle principle. Through intense envy or malice, the mind may at times be in a state of concentration, but this is not yogic concentration.

2. Stupefaction (mudha).

In this state of mind, obsession with a matter connected with the senses renders one unfit to think of subtle principles. An example is someone engrossed in thoughts of family or wealth to the point of infatuation.

3. Restlessness (vyagra).

This state is not to be equated with the *kshipta* state. Most spiritual devotees basically have this type of mind — a mind that may be calm sometimes and disturbed at other times. When temporarily calm, a restless mind may understand the real nature of subtle principles when it hears of them, and can contemplate them for an extended period. But although concentration is possible with a restless mind, it is not long-lasting. Liberation cannot be secured through concentration alone when the mind is habitually restless, because when concentration ceases, distraction arises again. Until the mind is free of distractions, and a permanent one-pointedness develops, the state of salvation is impossible to achieve.

4. One-pointedness (ekagra).

Patanjali, the compiler of the *Yoga Sutras*, has defined this as a state of mind wherein, on the fading away of one thought, another thought is in succession with the previous thought; and when a continuous succession of such states continues, the mind is called "one-pointed." Slowly it becomes a habit of the mind in waking consciousness, and even in the dream state. When one-pointedness is mastered, one attains *samprajnata samadhi*. This *samadhi* (bliss) is true yogic samadhi, leading to salvation.

5. Suppression (niruddha).

This is the state devoid of thought. By constant practice of the cessation of thoughts, one can truly understand the world of names and forms as a product of the mind. When the mind ceases to exist in a practical sense of the term, all else dissolves.

The mind normally functions through three different states:

- Waking consciousness
- Dream consciousness
- Deep sleep

In a state of waking consciousness, one works in coordination with the upper and lower brain and the twin hemisphers. In the dream state one is more dominated by the subconscious mind, the seat of which is the lower brain; as such, dreams become a tool of fulfillment of suppressed desires connected with the animal nature of man. Only those who have mastered the art of habitual one-pointedness are able to maintain it in the dream state. Habitual one-pointedness is the fruit of constant yogic discipline and self-restraint. When the aspirant achieves this state, he transcends the realm of the lower brain (the subconscious mind) and dwells in the state of blissfulness, samprajnata samadhi, an altered state of mind in which mental fluctuations and modifications are suppressed; this is the consciousness during deep sleep.

There is also a fourth state, the state of the fourth dimension. In yogic terminology this is *turiya*, the state of unconscious consciousness. Recently, modern practitioners of psychology have become interested in this state in which the conscious mind is suppressed, yet where complete consciousness exists. This state is also known as the "altered state of consciousness."

The science of Yoga serves to develop an atmosphere of peace and habitual one-pointedness. It leads toward unity in thought and action; prescribes devices for cleansing the mind; gives awareness; stops inner dialogue; and provides inner silence. It creates nonattachment; ensures better physical and mental health; offers guidance to the aspirant for adoption of a particular diet necessary for practicing disciplines and self-restraint; and it expands consciousness.

There are different kinds of yogic science, just as there are different kinds of human temperament.

1. Raja Yoga, the Yoga of meditation.

By suspension of the thinking principle, one is able to achieve union by will.

2. Jnana Yoga, the Yoga of true knowledge.

By the constant discrimination between the unreal and the real, one may achieve union through true knowledge.

3. Karma Yoga, the Yoga of selfless action.

This is action or duty for duty's sake, not for the pleasure-seeking nature, or the animal nature. Karma Yoga enables one to achieve union through service.

4. Bhakti Yoga, the Yoga of spiritual devotion.

One seeks union through devotion, love, and surrender.

5. Hatha Yoga, the Yoga of physical disciplines and restraint.

The aspirant of Hatha Yoga seeks union through psychophysical devices and through altered states of consciousness. Hatha Yoga is for aspirants who require physical training for specific strengths to achieve obstacle-free meditation.

Each of these yogic sciences in its own way approaches the same goals: unity of being; unity in thought and action; and unity of the internal and the external.

TANTRA YOGA

A combination of all of the above-mentioned yogic sciences, Tantra Yoga is a practical type of Yoga wherein the body and mind are considered to be one, and the body is believed to be a vehicle of the mind. According to this system the mind is abstract, the body concrete; to work with the abstract mind we need to use the concrete material stuff called *body*. It is in the body that the psychic centers are located. The functional aspect of the cerebrospinal system is called *the mind*. The spine is the seat of all responses. Tantra's basic principle is shakti (female power), which is manifested as matter and mind, though supreme consciousness is mindless. When there is no mind, there is no limitation, and man is then pure consciousness. To go beyond the mind, one stops its vehicle so that its activities become suspended. *Prana* (breath) is the mind's vehicle. *Apana* is prana that exists in the region extending from below the navel to the anus, and is responsible for all activities in the pelvic region, including ejaculation, urination, and defecation. If this prana, which is charged with negative ions, is made to function with apana and is forced to enter through the central canal in the spinal column, there is a fusion between the negative ions of prana and the positive ions of apana. This generates

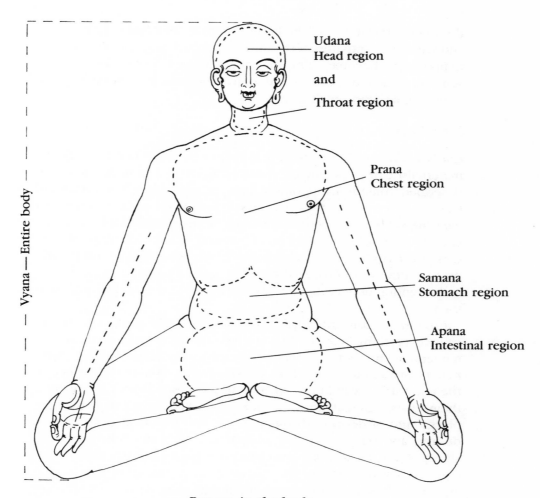

Udana
Head region

and

Throat region

Prana
Chest region

Samana
Stomach region

Apana
Intestinal region

Vyana — Entire body

Pranas in the body

great amounts of energy which, in turn, help in the ascent of the dormant energy that is at rest at the base of the spine — Kundalini. Before the generation of this energy is physically possible, the aspirant must become prepared through bodily purifications, *asana*s (yogic postures), *mudra*s (gestures), and *pranayama* (yogic breathing).

The system of working with the Kundalini is basically tantric in origin. It works through the union of the psyche with matter, and the mind with the physical body. In principle, the body plays a great role in producing various moods, including the highest mood, samadhi, the mood of bliss. This state is achieved by channeling energy through the nervous system and through the spine. The energy ascends through a narrow passage in the spinal column and passes through six psychic centers before it reaches its final abode, the seventh center. The seventh center is located in the cerebrum, the hollow space between the twin hemispheres of the brain, where again a fusion takes place, and where the activities of the mind are completely suspended. Both hemispheres become calm, the inner dialogue stops, one loses all sense of time and space, and identifications and false notions of the phenomenal world melt away.

The Chakras

Chakras are psychic centers that cannot be described fully from a materialistic or physiological standpoint. Just as a painting cannot be described from the standpoint of lines and curves or varying shades of paints — even though these can be said to form the basic structure of a painting — similarly, *chakras* can not be described in terms of psychology, physiology, or any other physical science. Chakras are centers of activity of subtle, vital force termed *sukshma prana* (subtle prana); they are interrelated with the parasympathetic, sympathetic, and autonomous nervous systems, and thus the gross body is related to them.

Chakra is a Sanskrit word that denotes circle and movement. Because everything in the body is of a circular shape and is constantly in movement, the centers of those movements are called *chakras. Chakra* is a word also used for *wheel*. Chakras can be thought of as wheels of the mind that dwell in the forest of desires. And desires, like wheels themselves, are great motivating forces. Each chakra is a stage-by-stage playground of desires. Throughout life one dwells in this forest of desires, and one thinks and understands life's situations from the standpoint of the chakra in which he normally feels most comfortable.

In discussing chakras we are necessarily discussing the subtle aspects of these centers. Nerves are merely vehicles, but the message is subtle and is not devoid of consciousness or self-consciousness. The connection between the gross and the subtle in the human organism is through intermediate conductors that are connected with the sense organs and work organs. Through Yoga one trains both types of organs to adopt a discipline and to help the body become a true asset. Yoga makes an aspirant the best friend of his own body, sense organs, and work organs, and creates coordination between the right and left sides of the body, which normally do not coordinate, but rather alternate. The Yoga that focuses specifically on the chakras and the dormant Kundalini energy is variously called Kundalini Yoga, Laya Yoga, Kriya Yoga, and Shaktipatamaha Yoga.

This book is about Tantra Yoga, and the figures drawn here are facsimiles of illustrated tantric texts. A description accompanies each chakra, and is simply an explanation of the figures drawn therein. These figures are a language in and of themselves, and aid the aspirant in remembering the chakras, which is an invaluable device for one trying to visualize chakras while meditating on them. Concentration on physical organs or spots in the body as prescribed by many spiritual masters is misleading, for the chakras are not material. The true aspirant is best advised to apply concentration to subtle centers in relation to each presiding consciousness. These centers have an ultimate relationship with the gross body and its physical functions. Diagrams of chakras enable the aspirant of Kundalini Yoga to meditate by coloring the drawings and simultaneously repeating the bija (seed) sounds and other sounds that are present in the lotus petals of the chakras.

One of the hemispheres in the human brain is visual, the other verbal. The visual hemisphere works with the visual images of the chakras presented in the illustrations that have been specially designed here for coloring. Simultaneously, the verbal hemisphere is engaged by sounds and seed sounds. Using the faculties of hearing and sight together is a form of Tantra. One who masters this practice will find himself or herself in a meditative state while neither inert nor inactive. One subtly receives inspiration from the forms and colors.

This book is an introduction to the classical understanding of chakras. Its roots are practical and of ancient origin, and still functionally practical today.

CHAPTER TWO

Kundalini

CHAKRAS, AS PREVIOUSLY MENTIONED, are not materially real, nor can they be described from a purely materialistic or physiological standpoint. Thus we must discuss the subtle aspects of these psychic centers, which work in coordination with nerves, cells, and fibers that are related through intermediate conductors with the gross system, the sense organs, and the work organs. It is important to explain, especially to those who wish to awaken Kundalini, that its material is the immobile support of all operations and activities in the body and, like consciousness, it has no organ. Kundalini maintains all the beings of the world by means of inspiration and expiration. Kundalini is a vital force.

The word *kundalini* comes from the *Sanskrit* word *kundal*, which means "coil." It is compared with a serpent that, while resting and sleeping, lies coiled. The comparison between a serpent and Kundalini comes because of the nature of its movement, which is spiraling and serpent-like. Kundalini is an aspect of the eternal, supreme consciousness, which is both with and without attributes. In the attributeless *(nirguna)* aspect it is the will of cosmic consciousness, and is pure consciousness. In the aspect with attributes *(saguna),* this energy is often personified as Kundalini, an aspect of the Great Goddess, just as primal energy, or shakti, is personified as Shakti. It is through the power of Kundalini that all creatures act. In individual bodies the same energy lies dormant, as a static center around which every form of existence revolves. In the phenomenal world there is always a power in and behind every activity, a static background.

Examination of Hatha Yoga and tantric scriptures reflects that Kundalini is energy in static and kinetic form, which is present in all manifested phenomena. The kinetic energy becomes the energy used by the phenomenon for its survival, and the static energy remains dormant during normal working consciousness. Whenever one becomes self-conscious and realizes that there is a higher purpose in life — that there is also another state of consciousness beyond the normal waking, sleeping, or dreaming states; whenever one's desires for sensual enjoyments are fulfilled; when one finds no attraction in the phenomenal world — then one experiences a state of nonattachment, of introversion. This withdrawal from indulgence opens doors to the inner world, and one experiences a light that leads one toward union, union between the duality of matter and mind.

At this time for total change the static energy, which is lying dormant, becomes kinetic and adopts a course that is contrary to the law of gravitation and passes through all the psychic centers located in the spine. The force that channels energy through the central canal comes from the fusion of the negative ions of prana with the positive ions of apana. The seat of apana is in the region below the navel, the pelvic area. Therefore the energy that is at rest in the base of the spine is in static form. This occurs where the upper bones of the coccyx and the lower bones of the sacrum join in a cluster of nerves appearing like a fibrous root. Traditionally, this is known as Muladhara Chakra, or the basal plexus. By following Hatha Yoga and performing *Laya Karma* (that is, *mudras* or gestures) and asanas, or postures, accompanied by meditation, mantra chanting, and visualization techniques, one is able to activate this latent energy that works with the autonomic nervous system and the parasympathetic nervous system, which are linked with the ganglia constituting the main plexi. The dormant energy is directed toward the highest place, the seventh chakra, which is described as the seat of consciousness. Here again, a fusion between positive and negative ions takes place. The force generated by such fusion creates a great illumination that destroys the ignorance of the mind, the primary cause of duality. One who experiences this state attains nondual consciousness and becomes enlightened. According to Hindu scriptures, the true yogi crosses the ocean of birth, disease, old age, and death.

When awakened, this dormant energy works through the *nadi*s. The word *nadi* comes from the Sanskrit root *nad*, meaning movement. In the Rigveda, the most ancient Hindu scripture, the word *nadi* means "stream." The concept of nadis is based on the understanding that they are channels; any channel through which anything flows is a nadi. Included in this concept of nadis are acupuncture meridians; streams of the cardiovascular system; lymphatic system streams; nerves; muscles; arteries; veins; the *manovahini*, or *manovaha* (the channel of mind); and the *chittavaha* (the channel of *chitta*, or being). Thus *nadi* can be translated as "vessel," "channel," "cord," "tube," or "duct."

According to the foregoing definition, there are two types of nadis:

- Subtle . . . invisible channels of subtle energy
- Gross . . . channels of subtle energy visible as cords, vessels, or tubes

This explanation gives a clear indication that nadis are not only nerves, but all kinds of channels, and this is the reason that the term "nerve" is not used for nadis in the texts of the Ayurveda, ancient Indian medicine. Tantric anatomy does not go into descriptions of the gross and subtle nervous systems. In the tantric tradition the universe is believed to be made up basically of two things: matter and energy, or, in another manner of speaking, the *saguna* ("with attributes") and the *nirguna* ("without attributes").

In Tantra, matter is treated as the vehicle of energy, and energy is considered to be conscious (not, however, that energy which is devoid of consciousness). This consciousness, when it becomes manifest, finds a vehicle for itself, which is *manas*, or the mind. Consciousness is fourfold. It is a combination of the following:

Manas . . . Mind
Buddhi . . . Intellect
Ahamkara . . . Identification ("is-ness")
Chitta . . . Being

While assuming physical forms, this consciousness exists in five *kosha*s, or sheaths, and operates through the physical body, the best vehicle for expression. These sheaths are:

Annamayi Kosha . . . Sheath of Matter
Pranamayi Kosha . . . Sheath of Vital Air
Manomayi Kosha . . . Sheath of Mind
Vijnanamayi Kosha . . . Sheath of Knowledge
Anandamayi Kosha . . . Sheath of Bliss

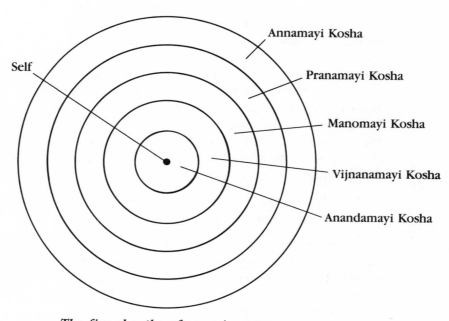

The five sheaths of consciousness

The physical body is composed of eight ingredients known as *mula prakriti*: (1) *manas* (mind); (2) *buddhi* (intellect); (3) *ahamkara* (ego/identification); and the five elements: (4) *akasha* (space/ether); (5) *vayu* (air); (6) *agni* (fire); (7) *apah* (water); and (8) *prithvi* (earth). The five elements form the three *dosha*s, or basic humors in the body:

Vayu . . . wind (from the air element)

Pitta . . . bile (from the fire element)

Kapha . . . mucos (from a combination of water and earth elements)

There are also three *gunas,* or qualities, that operate through the doshas:

Sattva (equanimity, lightness)

Rajas (passion)

Tamas (sloth, darkness)

Thus it is perceived that the entire octave of prakriti exists within the human organism (a well-known tantric adage is "as in the macrocosm, so in the microcosm"). The connecting force of this whole network is Vayu Prana, which operates through particular nadis — Pranavaha Nadi (carrier of pranic force), and Manovaha Nadi (carrier of mental force).

The Nadis

Nadis are linked with the chakras. The central canal, Sushumna, plays a vital role in yogic and tantric practices. Chakras are centers of interchange between physical and psychological energy within the physical dimension, and prana is the force that links the physical with the mental and the mental with the spiritual. In fact, the physical, the mental, and the spiritual are the same and work together on all levels. Some of the gross nadis, such as physical nerves, veins, and arteries, are known in modern medical science. But, as all nadi do not take a physical form, nor are visible in character, it is impossible to locate them, observe them, or trace their pathway through less subtle means. Subtle nadis are of two kinds:

Pranavaha Nadis . . . conduits of pranic force.

Manovaha Nadis . . . conduits of mental force.

Pranavaha and manovaha nadis generally run together. Although they defy description, they are somehow connected with the sensory nerves of the autonomic nervous system. Yoga nadis and nerves of the autonomic nervous system work together in the same way the psyche works with physiology.

Certain studies of anatomy contradict the description of Sushumna given by the tantric scriptures, stating that the central canal contains only cerebrospinal fluid, with no mention of the presence of nerve fibers. It is impossible neurologically for the spinal cord to have an opening at the top of the head for the inflow and outflow of prana. Therefore, it is difficult to provide an accurate anatomy of the chakras. In acupuncture there is a meridian called the Governor Vessel Meridian, which has some correspondence with Sushumna. In this meridian the energy flow starts at the tip of the coccyx, ascends the spine, reaches a point at the top of the head, and then courses down along the meridian line to a point just below the navel. Acupuncture meridians may be equated with pranavaha nadis.

According to the tantric treatise *Shiva Samhita*, there are fourteen principal nadis. Of these, Ida, Pingala, and Sushumna are considered the most important; all nadis are subordinate to Sushumna. Prana travels through Sushumna from the pelvic plexus to Brahma Randhra ("the cave of the *brahman*"; the hollow space between the two hemispheres of the brain), which is situated in the interior of the cerebrospinal axis. Muladhara Chakra is the meeting place of the three main nadis, and is known as Yukta Triveni (*yukta*, "combined"; *tri*, "three"; *veni*, "streams").

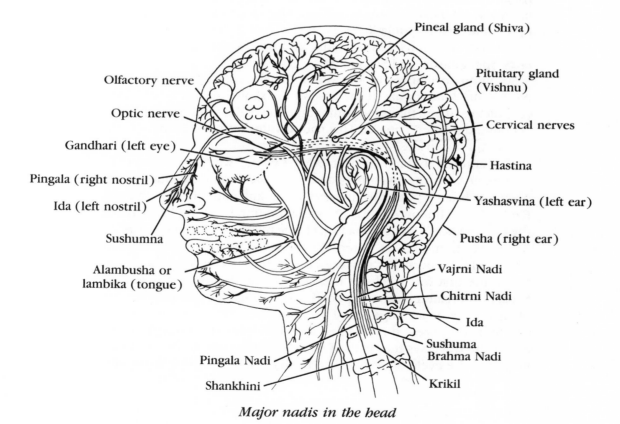

Major nadis in the head

The first ten nadis, according to the *Shiva Svarodaya*, are connected with the ten "gates," or openings, of the body:

1. Sushumna or Brahma Randha (fontanel)
2. Ida (left nostril)
3. Pingala (right nostril)
4. Gandhari (left eye)
5. Hastajihva (right eye)
6. Yashasvini (left ear)
7. Pusha (right ear)
8. Alambusha (mouth)
9. Kuhu (genitals)
10. Shankhini (anus)

1. Sushumna

Sushumna is centrally situated and passes through the meru danda (spinal column). According to V.G. Real*, it originates inside the *kanda* (fibrous material around which nerves interweave), which roughly corresponds with the level of the navel. This is contradictory, however, for most scriptures on Yoga, and specifically the *Shandilya Upanishad*, name Muladhara as the seat of Sushumna. The *Shiva Svarodaya* mentions 72,000 nadis, and names only three principal ones: Ida, Pingala, and Sushumna.

Sushumna originates in Muladhara Chakra, runs up the body and pierces the *talu* (palate at the base of the skull), and joins Sahasrara (the plexus of one thousand nadis at the top of the skull, known as the "Thousand-petaled Lotus"). This nadi divides into two branches: anterior and posterior.

The anterior branch goes to Ajna Chakra, which is situated in alignment with the eyebrows and joins the Brahma Randhra. The posterior branch passes from *behind* the skull and joins the Brahma Randhra. This hollow space is also known as Bhramara Gupha ("cave of the bumble bee"), and Andha Kupa ("the blind well," or tenth gate — see illustration, page 6). Externally this is the "soft spot" that is open when a child is born. In a newborn infant pulsation at this spot can be felt in the first few weeks of life; after the sixth month it begins to harden. Thereafter it can be opened only through the special practices of Laya Yoga, Svara Yoga, Kriya Yoga, or Nada Yoga. In the *shastra*s (ancient scriptures) it is said that one who leaves his body from the tenth gate traverses the "path of no return" (i.e., one achieves liberation from the cycle of death and rebirth). There are some yogis who

---

* *Mysterious Kundalini* (Bombay: Taraporavala Sons, 1928).

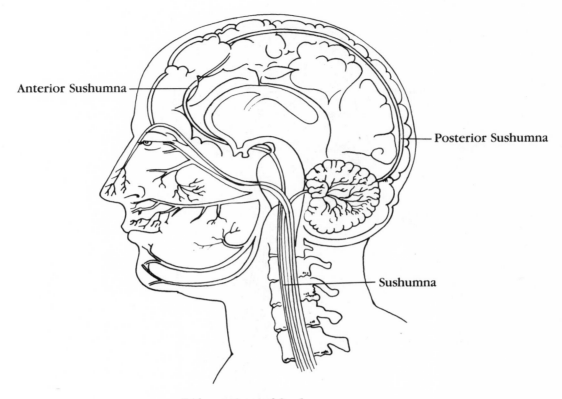

Anterior Sushumna

Posterior Sushumna

Sushumna

Bifurcation of Sushumna

observe disciplines to prepare the tenth gate so that their last breath will carry the soul through it to liberation. The true aspirant desirous of liberation will work with the posterior branch of Sushumna.

Another special feature of Sushumna is that it is not time-bound. When a yogi in meditation establishes himself at the midpoint between the eyebrows in the Ajna Chakra (third eye) and transcends the prana into the Brahma Randhra region, he is beyond time. He becomes *trikaladarshi* (knower of past, present, and future). In Ajna Chakra he goes beyond time, and death cannot touch him. Functions of the physical body come to a standstill and the process of aging is stopped. Just before death all human beings breathe the Sushumna breath, whereby both nostrils work simultaneously. It is said that death — with the exception of accidental death — is not possible when either the Ida or Pingala alone is dominant. That is, when the right nostril is operating solely, or when one's breath is predominantly in the left nostril, death does not occur.

Sarasvati Nadi and Brahma Nadi are also names for Sushumna. This is not a proper identification, however, for Sushumna is a channel wherein there are other *sukshma (subtle) nadis, and Sarasvati is a complementary nadi of Sushumna that flows outside of it on the left side.*

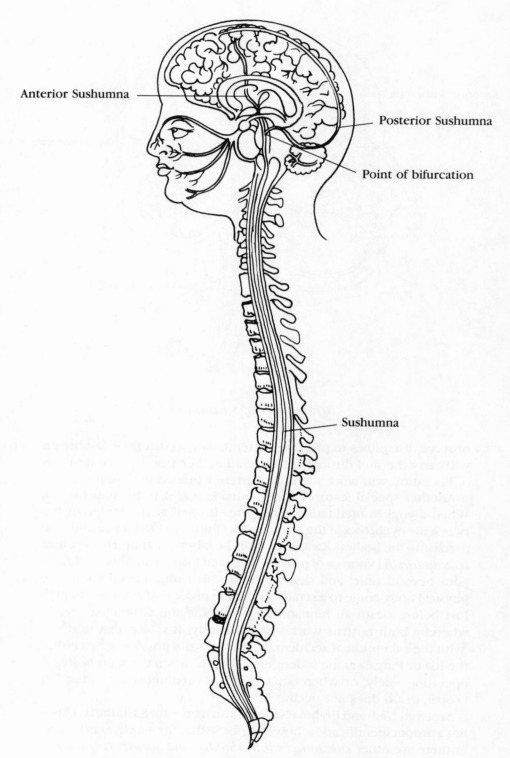

Anterior Sushumna

Posterior Sushumna

Point of bifurcation

Sushumna

Origin and termination of Sushumna

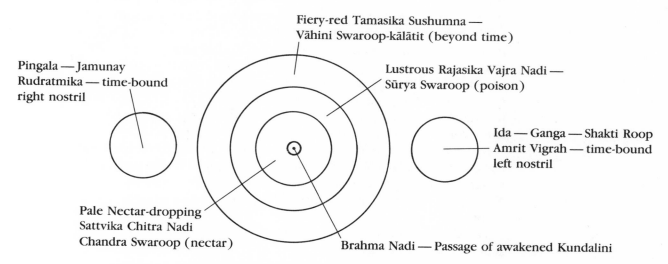

Fiery-red Tamasika Sushumna —
Vāhini Swaroop-kālātit (beyond time)

Lustrous Rajasika Vajra Nadi —
Sūrya Swaroop (poison)

Pingala — Jamunay
Rudratmika — time-bound
right nostril

Ida — Ganga — Shakti Roop
Amrit Vigrah — time-bound
left nostril

Pale Nectar-dropping
Sattvika Chitra Nadi
Chandra Swaroop (nectar)

Brahma Nadi — Passage of awakened Kundalini

Sushumna operates when both nostrils are active simultaneously.
It is also known by the name Saraswati. Through Sushumna the yogi enters eternity.

Cross section of Sushumna According to *Lalita Sahasranāma.*

According to the Lalita Sahasranama (a tantric text devoted to the
Goddess), the fiery-red *tamasika* Sushumna has within it a lustrous
rajasika Vajra Nadi, which is of the nature of the sun and poison, and a
pale nectar-dropping *sattvika* Chitra Nadi, which is of the nature of
the moon. This nadi is responsible for dreams, hallucinations, and
visions. *Chitra* in Sanskrit means a picture or painting. This nadi is
automatically active in painters, poets, and visionary artists. The end of
the Chitra Nadi is called Brahma Dvara ("the door of *brahman*"), and
Kundalini Devi ascends through this door to her final abode — the
Manasa Chakra, Lalana Chakra, or Soma Chakra — the meeting place of
Kameshvara and Kameshvari (Shiva and Shakti), which is just above
the spot where Kamadhenu (the wish-fulfilling cow) resides.

As mentioned above, Muladhara Chakra is the meeting place of the
three main nadis and is called Yukta Triveni (*yukta*, "involvement";
triveni, "meeting of three streams"). From Muladhara they move,
alternating at each chakra until they reach Ajna Chakra, where they
again meet, forming a gentle knot with Sushumna. Here the meeting of
the three streams is called Mukta Triveni (*mukta*, "liberated"). As the
sixth chakra (Ajna Chakra) is beyond the elements, the yogi who
achieves this level by his yogic power via Sushumna is freed from
bondage. Once established, the yogi maintains a state of *kevali kumbhaka* (ability to reduce the flow of breath). Beyond the knot in Ajna
Chakra, Ida and Pingala end in the left and right nostrils, respectively,
and thus Chitra and Vajra act as lunar and solar currents, and Brahma

Nadi acts as fiery *tamasika* Sushumna. The nadis Vajra and Chitra are interior solar and lunar currents of Sushumna. They are manovahi nadis, mentioned in the *Sushruta Samhita* and also by the Buddhist philosopher Vijnanabhikshu. A yogi seated in this chakra has become tattvatita (beyond the elements), but he is still subject to changes of mood created by the predominance of one or another guna (attribute, quality); he is not yet gunatita (beyond attributes). Once he is gunatita he attains *nirvikalpa samadhi* (also known as *nirbija*, or "seedless" *samadhi*) — a special state of deep and lasting meditation.

In the space outside the meru danda (spinal column), to the left and right, are the nadis Ida and Pingala. The substance of Sushumna Nadi, which is in the middle, is composed of threefold channels, the gunas. The nadis Vajra and Chitra begin at a point two fingerbreadths above Sushumna.

The triangle shown in the diagram on page 84 [Kameshvara Chakra] is composed of three nadis:

1. CAUSAL	Raudri	Bindu	Shiva	Para
2. PHYSICAL	Jyestha	Nada	Shiva-Shakti	Sthula
3. ASTRAL	Vama	Bija	Shakti	Sukshma

2. Ida

Ida is the left channel. Carrier of lunar currents, Ida is feminine in nature and the storehouse of life-producing, maternal energy. Ida is nourishing and purifying, and therefore it is also called Ganga (Ganges). It is sometimes represented as the left eye. In Svara Yoga it represents the "left" breath, that is, breath predominantly flowing in and out of the left nostril. *Left* is described in the Tantras as magnetic, female, visual, and emotional in nature. In the practice of Pranayama (yogic breathing), with the exception of surya bhedana pranayama, the *puraka* (inhalation) is commenced with the left nostril. This excites Ida Nadi, for Ida Nadi originates in the left testicle and ends in the left nostril. Specific left nostril breathing will excite Ida Nadi, and its nourishing chemicals will purify the body chemistry, a benefit of which is ease in meditation. The *Shiva Svarodaya* and the *Jnana Svarodaya* recommend that all important activities, especially those that give stability to life, are best done when Ida is in operation.

In the system of Svara Yoga, practitioners observe the custom of keeping the left nostril open during the day to balance the solar energy that is received during the daylight hours. Ida Nadi is sattvika in nature and, by keeping it operating during the day (which is dominated by rajasika energy), one can increase sattva, thereby creating a balance in oneself; one becomes more relaxed and more alert mentally. Ida Nadi is responsible for restoring energy to the brain. Ida is situated on the left side of the meru danda and has been misidentified as the chain of nerve ganglia connected with nerve fibers called the sympathetic cord. A close similarity exists, perhaps because the sympathetic system controls and influences respiration, and because respiration is connected with the nostrils; as there is a correlation between the chakra and endocrine glands, the exact definition has not been documented in Western medicine. Ida is neither a nerve nor a sympathetic cord; it is a manovahi nadi. In various folklores around the world, and especially in India, the moon (Sanskrit, *chandra*) is related to the psyche. In the *Purusha Sukta* it is said: "*Chandrama manaso jatah*," that is, "The moon was born from the manas of the Virata Purusha [Supreme Self]."

"Moon breath" (left nostril breath) in Svara Yoga is called *Ida*. Yogis identify Ida as being a pranavahini nadi, and claim it to be one of the most important manovahi nadis. Prana, with the help of Ida, is able to flow in and out of the left nostril. During the ascending moon cycle (from the new moon to the full moon), Ida is dominant for nine days in a fortnight at the time of sunrise and sunset. Locating this nadi with modern technical devices has thus far not proved possible, but the pranavahi aspect of Ida can clearly be felt through the effects of *svara sadhana* (following the Science of Breath), and by practicing pranayama.

3. Pingala

Pingala is the right channel. Carrier of solar currents, Pingala is masculine in nature, and a storehouse of destructive energy. It is known as *Yamuna*. In its own way, Pingala is also purifying, but its cleansing is like fire. Pingala is sometimes represented as the right eye. In Svara Yoga, Pingala represents the right breath, that is, breath flowing in and out of the right nostril. Right is electrical, male, verbal, and rational in nature. Pingala Nadi makes the physical body more dynamic and more efficient, and it is this nadi that provides more vitality and more male power. *Surya bhedana pranayama* (breathing to increase sun/right power) is performed to increase vigor, stamina, and solar energy. Surya bhedana pranayama is an exception in the realm of yogic breathing: in this pranayama, inhalation begins through the *right* nostril, thus exciting Pingala Nadi. In Svara Yoga it is clearly acknowledged that Pingala Nadi makes a male "pure male," just as Ida makes a female "pure female." Right nostril predominance is recommended for physical activities, temporary jobs, discussions, debates, and, indeed, duels.

The yogic practice of keeping the right nostril open at night, when solar energy is less strong, maintains a balance in a healthy organism.

Keeping Ida Nadi active during the day and Pingala Nadi active at night increases vitality and longevity. Pingala is rajasika (energetic) in nature, and keeping it active during the tamasika (lazy) hours of the night increases the wholistic health of the organism.

The sun, yogis say, is related to the eyes of Virata Purusha. According to the *Purusha Sukta*, "*Chakshore suryo ajayatah*," that is, "From the eyes comes the sun," meaning that from the eyes of Virata Purusha the sun was born. The eyes are vehicles of the sun. The eyes discriminate. The eyes — and the sun — are related to intellect and the rational brain. The night is a time for fantasy, and dominance of the rational side of the brain (right-nostril dominance) at night prevents one from burning off energy through fantasizing. Great thinkers use the night for contemplation. It is said that "when it is night for worldly people, it is day for yogis." Pingala, like Ida, is a manovahi and pranavahi nadi. Pingala is more active during the descending moon cycle (from full moon to new moon) and operates for nine days in a fortnight at the time of sunrise and sunset. Willful control over Ida and Pingala nadis can be achieved through the practice of Svara Yoga or the sadhana (disciplines) of pranayama. Pingala Nadi brings the energy down from the center of combustion of the brain where matter (oxygen and glucose) is converted into life-giving energy (prana). Various texts on Yoga and Ayurveda describe the breath that we inhale as residing in the chest region. In addition to this breath we inhale prana, or vital life force.

4. Gandhari.

Nadi Gandhari stretches from below the corner of the left eye to the big toe of the left foot. Tying a thread around the big toe of the left foot cures a stye on the left eye; tie the thread before sunrise and tie it loosely. Gandhari Nadi can be excited by practicing *baddha padmasana* (lotus posture), in which one holds the big toes. Specifically, the practitioner crosses the arms behind the back while sitting in the lotus posture and then grasps the big toe of the left foot with the right hand, and the big toe of the right foot with the left hand. Baddha padmasana energizes this manovaha nadi, which is used to carry psychic energy from the big toes to Ajna Chakra. Gandhari is situated by the side of Ida Nadi and helps support it. Psychic energy from the lower part of the body is brought through Gandhari Nadi and its companion, Nadi Hastajihva.

5. Hastajihva

Hastajihva stretches from below the corner of the right eye to the big toe of the left foot. It is also a complementary nadi to Ida, and the three together — Gandhari, Ida, and Hastajihva — form the left channel.

The *Shiva Svarodaya* describes the termination point of Hastajihva as being in the right eye, although the *Jabal Upanishad* (named after Satyakam Jabal) maintains that the termination point is in the left eye.

6. *Yashasvini*

Yashasvini stretches from the right big toe to the left ear.

7. *Pusha*

Pusha stretches from the left big toe to the right ear. This nadi, along with Yashasvini Nadi, forms the right channel and is complementary to Pingala.

8. *Alambusha*

Alambusha begins at the anus and terminates in the mouth.

9. *Kuhu*

Kuhu begins in the throat and terminates in the genitals. In tantric practices, when one tries to raise his seminal fluid from the genitals to Soma Chakra, Kuhu Nadi serves as a carrier of the *bindu* (essence of the seminal fluid) and the aspirant becomes *urdhvareta* (one who can direct his seminal fluid upward). Practitioners of an exercise known as vajrauli are able to master this nadi. One who is able to master nadis can attain the highest states of consciousness and gain the powers known as *siddhi*s ("perfections"), which enable a yogi to have full command over the tattvas and gunas. This particular practice is for the male aspirant. He begins by sucking water up through the *lingam* (male genital organ). Milk is added to the water, and once the aspirant is able to suck pure milk, he may advance to the stage where he is able to absorb oil, which is heavier than milk. The next step is mastery over the ingestion of pure mercury. During these processes the aspirant develops his potential to work with prana, and when he advances to the point where he can suck mercury through his lingam, he will then be able to draw in his own seminal fluid, along with the vaginal fluid from his female counterpart. This ultimate practice brings him into a state of samadhi through the union of opposites (the two fluids) inside his own physical body.

10. *Shankhini*

Shankhini originates in the throat and moves between Sarasvati and Gandhari nadis on the left side of Sushumna Nadi, terminating in the anus. Shankhini Nadi becomes active through *vasti* (enema) or Ganesha Kriya (rinsing the anus). These two practices have great medicinal value; they should be learned through the instruction of a yoga teacher adept in them.

Four other nadis are considered to complete the list of basic currents in the body:

11. Sarasvati Nadi

Sarasvati Nadi is seated on the tongue. In India it is a common saying that Sarasvati, the goddess of speech, knowledge, and the fine arts, lives on the tongue, and that once a day she expresses herself in all human beings; whatever one says at that time becomes true. By observance of disciplines and purification, this nerve becomes active and eventually whatever one says is called into being, that is, it becomes true. The end of the tongue is in the throat, and therefore it is sometimes said that Sarasvati resides in the throat, in particular, the vocal cords, the physical organ of speech. Sarasvati Nadi is camphor white in color and lunar in nature; it runs parallel to Sushumna and is a complementary channel.

12. Payasvini Nadi

Payasvini Nadi flows between Pusha and Sarasvati nadis. Pusha is complementary to Pingala on the right side, and to Sarasvati (which is complementary to Sushumna) on the left. On its right side Payasvini Nadi is complementary to Sushumna because its termination point is located in the right ear. Ancient iconography depicts deities, sages, and *avatara*s (incarnations of the divine Self) as wearing spectacular earrings. These ornaments served a special purpose. A certain part of the earlobe is connected with cranial nerves and a pure metal earring inserted at this point gives the system access to ions and static electricity from the environment. Thus yogis, by piercing the ears and inserting earrings, are able to activate Payasvini Nadi. Even today, tantrics known as Kanphata yogis (belonging to the Nath sect of yogis) wear large hooped earrings.

13. Varuni Nadi

Varuni Nadi is situated between Yashasvini and Kuhu nadis. Varuni Nadi is a pranavaha nadi that helps to purify the *mala*s (toxins) in the lower trunk area. Varuni Nadi terminates at the anus. This nadi can be activated through water purification and by practicing vasti and Ganesha Kriya. When Varuni Nadi is not flowing properly, Apana Vayu (the wind or air that resides in the lower trunk) can become disturbed, causing an increase in tamas. In arousing Kundalini, this apana moves upward to the region of *samana*, where prana meets it and combustion between the negative charges of prana and positive charges of apana takes place. This generates great force and causes Kundalini to ascend through the Brahma Nadi. Varuni Nadi pervades the whole area of the lower torso and assists in keeping Apana Vayu free of toxins. Apana Vayu and Varuni Nadi together help in the process of excretion.

14. *Vishvodara*

Vishvodara flows between Kuhu and Hastajihva nadis and resides in the area of the navel. Vishvodara Nadi can be energized by the yogic exercises nauli kriya and uddiyana bandha, which involve contracting the rectal/abdominal muscles. Vishvodara Nadi is related to the adrenal glands and the pancreas, and, together with Varuni Nadi, improves the distribution and flow of prana throughout the body, especially the prana that rises through Sushumna Nadi.

Scriptures on Yoga mention many other minor nadis, but the above-mentioned fourteen are the major ones, and of these, ten are most important. These ten are related to what are called in Tantra the ten gates, and at death, one's vital force exits from *one* of the ten. These ten gates are manovahi nadis, or yoga nadis. Their correspondence with the sympathetic nervous system and with acupuncture meridians can be expressed because both of these systems operate with the help of pranic currents. Acupuncture meridians are pranavaha nadis and it is prana that makes the sympathetic and parasympathetic nervous systems work.

When Kundalini-energy rises, all the manovahi nadis become active. And when the combustion of prana and apana takes place, Kundalini Shakti is withdrawn with great force through Brahma Nadi and, piercing all the chakras, she reaches her abode in Soma Chakra for final union. The shastras describe Kundalini Shakti at that time as moving in different styles, depending upon the dominance of the elements in the person:

1. Ant-like movement	A creeping sensation is felt in the spine when the earth element *prithvi* is dominant. The sensation is concentrated at the base of the spine.
2. Frog-like movement	Hopping-and-stopping, and hopping again is the sensation one feels in the spine when the water element *apah* is dominant. A throbbing sensation is also felt: now strong, now weak.
3. Serpent-like movement	A feeling of excessive heat or of fire is felt in the area of the navel when the fire element *agni* is dominant. The sensation of the rising of a fiery stream

	in the spine is experienced. It is in the fire element that Kundalini is sometimes experienced as terrifying fiery energy.
4. Bird-like movement	A feeling of levitation, lightness, weightlessness, or the feeling of a sweeping, nice floating movement is felt in the spine when the air element *vayu* is dominant. The movement is regular and the feeling is often in the region of the heart. A vision of light may be experienced in the heart region, or a cold sensation in the spine may be felt.
5. Monkey-like movement	A feeling of jumping is experienced when *akasha* (space/ether element) is dominant. In this state Kundalini moves with such force that many chakras are crossed in one leap. In akasha the movement is not as steady as in the earth element, not as fluid as in the water element, and not as fiery as in the fire element. It comes like a storm, and in no time it ascends to the highest center.

The Knots

When Kundalini reaches Ajna Chakra, one is beyond the tattvas, or elements, and is established in one's own self. Danger of falling back into the trap of emotional ups and downs ends. In tantric terminology, the "three knots" —

Brahma Granthi (Knot of Brahma)

Vishnu Granthi (Knot of Vishnu)

Rudra Granthi (Knot of Rudra, or Shiva) —

are now untied. Phenomenal reality becomes pervaded by divine energy, and the self becomes established in the Sheath of Bliss (Anandamayi Kosha).

Brahma Granthi is the first knot and is located in the first chakra, the Muladhara. Although this is the location depicted in the *Jabal Upanishad* and the *Yogashikha Upanishad*, some tantric scriptures

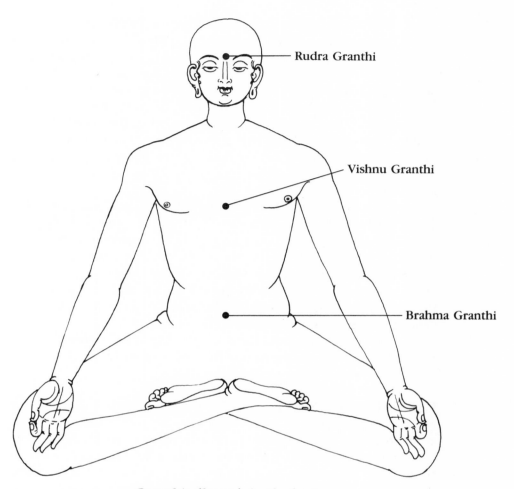

Granthis (knots) in the body

place the Brahma Granthi in the area of the navel, because this is the knot of samsara, the world of "names and forms" (nama-rupa). The world of names and forms presents the first obstacle in the growth of the spiritual aspect of the individual self, or *jiva.* Agni Tattva (the fire element), which is a product of the subcategory called the Rupa ("form") Tanmatra, is located here. This knot presents the first obstacle in the ascent of Kundalini, and it obstructs Kundalini's path as she begins to move toward the higher centers. Brahma is the creator of this world of names and forms — and therefore this knot is called the Knot of Brahma.

This world of names and forms enters us through five sense organs (eyes, ears, nose, tongue, and skin), which in tantric language are called the "five windows." This world occupies a great deal of our consciousness — it creates ambitions and desires — and traps the mind. Untying this knot frees one from the bondages caused by attachment, and as long as one does not untie this knot one cannot meditate effectively. This knot creates restlessness and prevents the mind from becoming one-pointed *(ekagra)*. By closing the five windows through the constant practice of pratyahara (willful withdrawal of sense organs), one can master the mind. When the body chemistry becomes pure by the practice of nadi shodhana, the energy rises — and one can untie the knot. Before this can be attained, however, the five *yama*s and *niyama*s, or "restraints," should be practiced, and one should achieve a stable *asana* (posture) in which he can sit for an extended period of time.

Once the aspirant has become adept at nadi shodhana and pratyahara, meditation on the chakras can begin. Starting with the first chakra, one should practice visualization by reconstructing the chakra drawings in the mind. All this should be done in a suitable natural environment in the presence of an experienced guru who is properly initiated — and whose presence produces calmness and stillness in the mind. Faith in the guru — and the grace of Kundalini Devi — can produce miracles, and the knot can be untied. After Kundalini passes through and properly unties the Knot of Brahma, the aspirant of Yoga becomes centered, and the images from the world of names and forms do not interrupt the meditation.

Vishnu Granthi is located in the area of Anahata Chakra (heart chakra), and presents the next obstacle in the path of Kundalini. This knot produces *karuna* ("compassion"), attachment to the cosmic Good, and a keen desire to help suffering humanity. This attachment to compassion makes one bound to spiritual organizations and orders. Vishnu is the lord of preservation, and Vishnu Granthi is the knot that creates the desire to preserve ancient knowledge, traditions, institutions, and spiritual orders. This attachment is further strengthened and inspired by the heart chakra — the chakra of devotion, faith, and love. But even the devotion to scriptural knowledge and the respect for spiritual orders becomes a bond. Only by true discrimination, knowledge, and faith can one untie the Knot of Vishnu and realize the purpose behind the cosmos, which is a part of the divine plan. This realization takes one beyond the attachment of preservation. One can become liberated from the traditional bonds that are deep-seated within the genetic code of each aspirant. Through Yoga it is possible to transcend the genetic code to complete freedom (svatantrya). After untying the Knot of Brahma one moves beyond the attachment to the world of names and forms — and after untying the Knot of Vishnu one moves beyond the attachments caused by emotional ties to traditions and commitments that appear as loyalty to a particular order. The individual ego dissolves here and the will of God prevails. One no longer feels responsible to the particulars of the world of names and

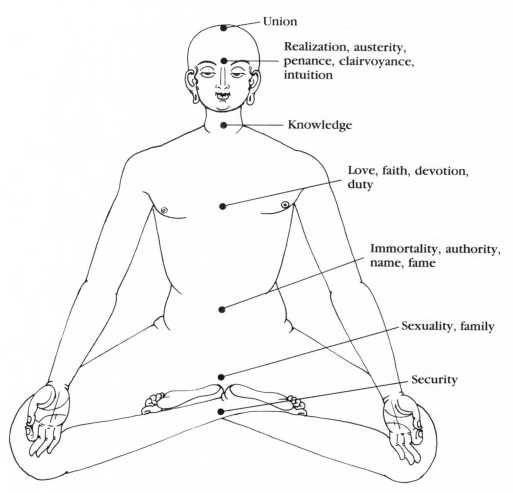

Union

Realization, austerity, penance, clairvoyance, intuition

Knowledge

Love, faith, devotion, duty

Immortality, authority, name, fame

Sexuality, family

Security

Desires and Obstacles

forms, fully comprehending its illusory nature. One understands *lila* (divine play) and acts out his role without further creating seeds of *karma*s that will bring one back to this world of maya. One begins to hear *anahad naad (anahata nada,* the cosmic sound) and *shruti*s (cosmic frequencies); shrutis are heard by yogis and then delivered to the world in the form of mantras; organized as a unit, the shrutis constitute the body of the Veda.

As stated above, Vishnu Granthi is difficult to untie because of its connection with the genetic code. This is one reason for the creation of the institution of asceticism called *sannyasa* in India. By entering this order one becomes dead in the social sense; his new birth begins in a spiritual order, and he is called "twice-born." The family of the person entering sannyasa is supposed to perform all of his funerary rites. This enables the aspirant to free himself from the deep ties of genetic code. Initiation given to the aspirant at this time helps him to untie the Vishnu Granthi.

Rudra Granthi is located in the area of the third eye. This is the last knot — and after untying it the aspirant established himself in the Sheath of Bliss. After annihilating the world of names and forms, one must destroy the remaining attachments that obstruct the path of the Kundalini on its way to Soma Chakra. When Kundalini ascends Vishuddha Chakra and reaches Ajna Chakra, the aspirant, who is now a yogi, becomes *tattvatita*, that is, beyond the five elements of earth, water, fire, air, and akasha. From the tattvas the whole world of names and forms evolves — and in tattvas it dissolves. It is tattvas that continuously change the chemical makeup of the physical body and bring emotional fluctuations and attachments in the individual self. After crossing the fifth chakra Kundalini moves to the sixth, where the tattvas merge into their source, the Mahat or Maha Tattva. Here the Ida and Pingala nadis cross over each other and disintegrate in the left and right nostrils, respectively. As lunar and solar channels, Ida and Pingala are time-bound. After this plexis in Ajna Chakra, the time-bound consciousness dissolves, and the yogi establishes himself in infinity. This knot then unties itself, and the yogi is able to ascend with his moving energy into Soma Chakra.

It is stated in tantric scriptures that when a yogi reaches Ajna Chakra he achieves the power to see the past, present, and future very clearly. He becomes *trikaladarshi* (*tri*, "three"; *kala*, "time"; *darshi*, "seer") or *trikalajna* ("knower of past, present, and future"), that is, a visionary. He can clearly see what is happening anywhere, at any time, and has the power to be present in any place at any time. The barriers of time and space do not exist for him anywhere. But it is at this point that Rudra Granthi becomes an obstacle, for the yogi can become lost in his intuitive power, siddhis, and miracles. If the yogi does not pay attention to such visions and goes beyond attachment to the siddhis, he is able to progress — and to transcend the three gunas, becoming *gunatita* (beyond the aspects or qualities), establishing himself in eternal bliss, complete union, and nondual consciousness.

In summary, Brahma Granthi is related to the physical body and to the world of names and forms. Vishnu Granthi is related to the astral body and to the world of emotions. Rudra Granthi is related to the causal body and to the world of thought, ideas, visions, and intuitions.

During the process of working through the knots the yogi listens to ten kinds of sounds that help him to achieve a state of deep meditation:

1. The chirping of birds
2. The sound of crickets
3. The sound of bells

4. The sound of the conch
5. The sound of the *vina* (Indian lute)
6. The sound of the *mridanga* (barrel drum)
7. The sound of the flute
8. The sound of the *pakhavaj* (another type of drum)
9. The sound of the trumpet
10. The roar of a lion

HOW TO AWAKEN KUNDALINI

The primary prerequisite for awakening this sleeping energy is purification of the body: cleansing of the nerves and purification of the mind. Purification is a device to free the entire system of accumulated toxins. Because the body and the mind always work in coordination with each other, purification of the body helps that of the mind, and vice versa.

Purification of the Body

There are many ways in which the body can be deeply cleansed. Some devices are common to many different cultures; various medical sciences have their own methods. Ayurveda, the Indian science of medicine, prescribes fasting as the most effective method. Three days of fasting on lukewarm water only cleanses the body of toxins and cures disorders without medicines. Hatha yoga presents a well-defined system known as *kshata karma*s (kshata, "six"; *karma*, "act"), or "six acts of purification." These were devised by Hatha yogis to purify the body and mind simultaneously. The kshata karmas are:

1. *Dhauti*
2. *Vasti*
3. *Neti*
4. *Trataka*
5. *Nauli*
6. *Kapalabhati*

When properly guided and administered, these six acts of purification are very effective. They are best performed in a clean, quiet place, and it is strongly recommended that they be done under the guidance of an adept master of these acts. The actual techniques of the kshata karmas, yogis advise, should be kept secret among yogic initiates.

1. Dhauti — Throat Cleansing.

Take a strip of natural cotton cloth four fingerbreadths wide and fifteen spans long, according to the instructions of the master. (One span equals the length of the hand from the forefinger to the wrist. Individual span measurement is accurate in these exercises, as it differs from person to person; one thus uses one's own measuring span.) A long strip of soft, new, muslin cloth would serve well. Wet it with warm water, swallow it slowly, and then draw it out slowly and gently. Begin by swallowing one span the first day, and increase daily by one span in length. Make sure the cloth is warm when swallowing it.

Dhauti practice takes fifteen days. Persons suffering from diseases caused by phlegm may extend the practice. Dhauti cleans the alimentary canal, cures bronchial diseases, asthma, diseases of the spleen, skin diseases, and all diseases caused by phlegm.

2. Vasti — Anal/Lower Intestinal Tract Cleansings.

Take a piece of smooth, fresh bamboo about six fingerbreadths long and about one and one-half fingerbreadths in diameter. Apply some butter to make it smooth. Sit in a bathtub with water reaching the navel. Assume *utkatasana* (sit on the haunches, balancing the body on the toes) and insert the tube about four fingerbreadths into the anus. Contract the anus to draw in water. Shake the water internally and then expel it. Repeat many times.

Vasti cleanses the lower intestinal tract. It increases the appetite and the "stomach fire" (i.e., digestive power), and may cure enlargement of glands and the spleen, dropsy and other stomach diseases, and all diseases arising from excess wind, bile, and phlegm. Proper practice of vasti refines one's constitution, sense organs, and internal organs.

3. Neti — Nasal/Sinus Cleansings.

Take a piece of thread without knots. Smooth it with *ghee* (clarified butter). Place one end of the thread into one nostril and, closing the other nostril with one finger, inhale through the open nostril and exhale through the mouth. By repeating this process the thread will be inhaled into the throat. Gently pull the thread. Repeat the process, beginning with the opposite nostril. Now it will be possible to place the thread in one nostril and draw it out through the other. Thus the process is complete.

Neti purifies the nasal passages, the sinuses, the frontal lobe and the front part of the skull. It stimulates the whole nervous system, increases vision, and enables one to perceive subtle things through the eyes. Neti is also performed by drinking water up through the nostrils and spitting it out through the mouth. This is called *jala neti*.

4. Trataka — Eye Cleansing Exercise.

Trataka is a yogic practice of gazing with fixed eyes on a minute object without blinking and with complete concentration until tearing occurs. When the tears flow, close the eyes and visualize the after-image until it vanishes.

Through trataka one achieves one-pointedness of mind. Trataka helps cure diseases of the eyes, and enhances growth and development of the pineal gland. It also develops "witness consciousness," a state of watching one's internal and external actions without emotional involvement.

5. Nauli — Adominal Exercise.

This kriya (exercise) is the crown of Hatha Yoga. It is difficult and requires much practice. In the beginning it may seem impossible, but through constant willpower nauli can be mastered.

Leaning slightly forward, stand with feet apart and the hands resting on the knees. Expel all the air from the lungs. Contract the abdominal muscles, pulling them up inside as much as possible. Two nadis (nerves) will show prominence. Rotate them with the abdominal muscles to the right and to the left with the speed of a fast-circling eddy. Breathe in after the rotation. Repeat several times.

Nauli stimulates gastric fire; increases digestive power; induces joy; balances disorders created by wind, bile, and mucus; increases skin glow; and stimulates the nervous system.

6. Kapalabbati — Bellows-breathing Exercise.

Breathe in and out quickly and uniformly, like the bellows of a black-smith. Stop as soon as any strain is felt. Kapalabhati destroys all diseases caused by phlegm.

These are the kshata karmas prescribed in the system of Hatha Yoga. Another, separate purification exercise is also prescribed in Hatha Yoga. *Gaja karni* is performed by drawing up apana to the throat and vomiting any substances (food, water, etc.) that are present in the stomach. Gradual practice of this stomach cleansing brings the breath and all of the nadis under control.

Purification of the Mind*

The system of yoga prescribes an eight-fold path for the purification of the mind. The *Hatha Yoga Pradipika*, the major treatise on Hatha Yoga, delineates the stages of this path as follows:

1. *Yama*
2. *Niyama*
3. *Asana*

---

* For further background on this material, see appendix.

4. *Pranayama*
5. *Pratyahara*
6. *Dharana*
7. *Dhyana*
8. *Samadhi*

1. Yama.

The ten yamas are nonviolence, truth, honesty, sexual continence, forbearance, fortitude, kindness, straight-forwardness, moderation in diet, and purity (bodily cleansing). Making a habit of constantly practicing yamas purifies words, thoughts, and deeds.

2. Niyama.

The ten niyamas are austerity, contentment, belief in God, charity, worship of God, listening to explanation of doctrines/scriptures, modesty, having a discerning mind, repetition of prayers, and sacrifice/performing religious sacrifices. Constant practice of the niyamas creates a spiritual attitude and awakens one's witness consciousness. Through application of these disciplines the mind is automatically weaned from unnecessary attachment to worldly objects, and one is able to concentrate.

3. Asana.

Asanas are postures (literally, "seated postures"). There are eighty-four such postures described in Hatha Yoga, but all postures are not prescribed at all times, nor in all situations. The spine is kept straight, the head and neck are erect and in alignment. The body should be comfortably motionless. Correct posture has an equalizing effect, stilling the forces present in the body and slowing the breath rate and blood circulation; it makes one firm and steady, it facilitates meditation, and it helps cure diseases and fickleness of mind. Some asanas activate various nerve centers and help the body secrete growth hormones and produce antibodies. When the aspirant is able to sit in one posture steadily and comfortably for a long time, there is a movement of energy in higher centers. Through the steadiness of the asana the mind becomes steady.

Padmasana (lotus posture) and *siddhasana* are two highly praised asanas. For acquiring mastery of an asana, Patanjali offers two suggestions: (1) hold the physical posture in an immovable position for long periods, gradually mastering the posture through will, and (2) meditate on the infinite lord, who holds and balances the earth as the great serpent Shesha.

4. Pranayama.

Pranayama means control of prana. Prana, as discussed above, is the magnetic current of breath. It is the vehicle of the mind, which cannot function without it. Therefore consciousness, expressing itself through the mind, cannot perceive or function without prana. It maintains equilibrium in the body and provides vital force.

Deep breathing is not the same as pranayama, although it does promote health to a reasonable extent. The beneficial effects from deep breathing are due to the increased intake of oxygen, which influences the prana in the body. Real pranayama begins when the breath is held for some time between inhalation and exhalation. Inhalation is called *puraka*; holding the breath is called *kumbhaka*; and exhalation is called *rechaka*. Kumbhaka affects the flow of pranic currents in a very fundamental manner. After becoming well versed in pranayama the aspirant may direct the pranic currents through the central canal of the spinal column to promote the rise of Kundalini. The period of retention of breath must be prolonged gradually and cautiously. Alternate breathing affects the pranic currents, cleans subtle pranic channels (nadis), opens Sushumna, cools the right and left hemispheres of the brain, suspends activities of the brain and mind, and temporarily stops inner dialogue. Pranayama prepares the mind for the practice of visualization and concentration.

5. Pratyahara.

Pratyahara is withdrawal from sensory perceptions, thus breaking all connections with the outside world. Pratyahara appears to be control of the senses by the mind, but the real technique is withdrawal of the mind into itself. When an aspirant becomes completely absorbed in work, he or she forgets the world outside because the mind is completely absorbed. The sense organs do not register any signals coming from without. This example is an attempt to explain that withdrawal of the mind and sense organs is possible. All that is needed is deep concentration, coupled with complete absorption.

Constant practice of pratyahara brings about internalization of the mind; the senses become still and renounce their craving for objects. This practice affords the aspirant supreme mastery over the senses.

6. Dharana.

Dharana is concentration, stilling the mind and fixing it at one point. Traditionally the heart has been recognized as the principle region for fixation of the mind, the heart being the center or seat of individual consciousness, which is Sanskrit is called *jiva*. The brain is the center of the mind and senses, and the heart the center of life. The brain can stop functioning (as in samadhi), but if the heart is *completely* stopped, life cannot be sustained.

In Kundalini Yoga the heart is considered to be in the fourth, and central, chakra; three chakras are below the heart chakra and three are above it. In dharana each chakra becomes a point for fixing the mind. Concentration on each chakra should be performed sequentially, starting from the first, or Muladhara, chakra, and gradually approaching the seventh, Sahasrara, the seat of consciousness. This practice creates habitual one-pointedness of mind. Each chakra is related to one or another of the five elements, and fixing the mind on each center helps the aspirant concentrate on the elements. This concentration on the elements also helps the mind to become one-pointed. Fixing the mind, however, is not the final goal and thus is only a means of achieving deep, unbroken meditation, which is called *dhyana.*

7. *Dhyana.*

Dhyana is uninterrupted meditation without an object. In the previous stage, dharana, one concentrates on a desired object, image, chakra, or center. By continuous practice of dharana the mind becomes calm and the aspirant is able to achieve true meditation. When it becomes truly fixed, the mind loses consciousness of itself and becomes still. A continuous flow of energy in the spine is felt, and there is a calmness uninterrupted by thoughts or inner dialogue. It is in the state of *dhyana* that the inner dialogue stops.

In *dharana* one concentrates on chakras; in *dhyana* one meditates, and consciousness of the chakras vanishes. In dharana there are occasional distractions in the mind. Even the visualization of chakras causes distraction. But in dhyana this visualization ceases. Calmness of mind is experienced and a state void of thought prevails. It is here that the experience of bliss begins. The consciousness now enters the fourth state — beyond the three normal states of wakefulness, dreaming, and deep sleep. This is categorized as an "altered state of consciousness" in modern psychological terms and is called turiya by yogis. As the fruit of dharana is dhyana, the fruit of dhyana is samadhi.

8. *Samadhi.*

The term *samadhi* is formed from the three components *sam* (equal, balanced, complete), *a* (eternal), and *dhi* (*buddhi*, cognition, or knowledge). When the state of complete equilibrium is achieved, there is samadhi. For individual consciousness, samadhi is self-realization — free of awareness of the self, of time, or of space. By regular practice of pratyahara one achieves habitual withrawal of the mind from the realm of sense perception and fluctuations. The mind learns to internalize and become absorbed into itself. In its unnatural course the mind creates duality and, with the withdrawal of the mind, this duality ends. When all mental modifications are dissolved, the consciousness (which has been conditioned by these modifications) achieves its natural state of nonduality.

Consciousness is infinite; the mind makes it appear finite. Through the mind, consciousness becomes imprisoned in the individual consciousness of "I," "me," and "mine." Pratyahara helps the individual consciousness bring about a central state of mind by developing in it a habit of withdrawal from the phenomenal world. Through dharana, the mind is fixed and stilled. Through dhyana, the mind achieves tranquility. When this tranquility becomes a habit of mind it enters into the Sheath of Bliss and remains submerged in the ocean of nebulous bliss and knowledge.

According to Kundalini Yoga, samadhi is the union of Shakti, the female principle, with Shiva, the male principle. The seat of Shakti, called Kundalini Shakti, is the Muladhara Chakra (the pelvic plexus), and the abode of Shiva is Sahasrara Chakra (situated in the cerebrum). Kundalini sleeps in the Muladhara Chakra. When the yearning for self-realization comes in the aspirant — and he or she follows the eight-fold path (after proper purification of nerves, recital of seed sounds, and visualizations) — Kundalini awakens and ascends through the second, third, fourth, fifth, and sixth chakras, and reaches Sahasrara Chakra to unite with her lord, Kameshvara, the "lord of love." This union bestows infinite bliss on the aspirant and opens the doors to divine knowledge.

The Bandhas

Bandhas are devices to lock the areas where energy is temporarily contained so that it may be directed in the way that the yogi desires. There are three bandhas that open Sushumna and awaken Kundalini.

1. Mula Bandha.

This bandha can be performed by pressing the perineum with the left heel and placing the right foot upon the left thigh. The *sadhaka* (practitioner) should then contract the anus, drawing apana upward. By contraction of the Muladhara, apana (whose course is downward) is forced to go upwards, through Sushumna. Pressing the anus with the heel, the sadhaka then forcibly compresses the air, repeating the process until apana moves upward. Through this practice prana and apana unite and go into Sushumna. When apana rises and reaches the region of the navel, it increases the gastric fire. Apana, now combined with the fire of Manipura Chakra (the third chakra), pierces through

Anahata Chakra (the fourth chakra), where it mixes with the prana whose seat is in the region of the heart and lungs. Prana is hot in nature, and this heat further increases because of the fusion of the negative ions of prana and the positive ions of apana. This process awakens Kundalini.

According to tantric scriptures, it is through this extreme heat that the sleeping Kundalini is awakened, just as a serpent struck by a stick hisses and straightens itself. Then, like a snake entering its hole, Kundalini enters Sushumna. Yogis therefore make mula bandha a regular practice.

2. *Uddiyana Bandha.*

The literal meaning of *uddiyana* in Sanskrit is "flying up." The yogi forms this lock so that the great bird of prana will fly up through Sushumna incessantly. To perform this bandha the aspirant draws the abdominal muscles above and below the navel region so that they are pulled back toward the spine and up toward the heart. This can be accomplished by first expelling all the air present in the abdominal region, exhaling as fully as possible; withdrawal of the abdominal muscles is thereby facilitated. According to the shastras this bandha rejuvenates the body. It is called "the lion that kills the elephant of death." An aging sadhaka can become youthful through regular practice of uddiyana bandha. It takes about six months of regular practice to master the art of uddiyana bandha, after which prana begins to flow upward through Sushumna, reaching Sahasrara Chakra. This action brings about the last fusion in the Thousand-petaled-lotus Chakra, and at this point the sadhaka automatically achieves the state of samadhi.

3. *Jalandhara Bandha.*

This bandha is performed by contracting the throat and then placing the chin firmly in the hollow spot between the chest and the neck (approximately eight fingerbreadths above the chest). This cuts off circulation of the fluids from the head, and an independent circuit is established. There is a network of subtle nadis at this juncture, and through this bandha the downward flow of fluids from the cavity of the palate is arrested.

The fluid that flows from the cavity of the palate is described as *soma* (nectar, or elixir). This cerebrospinal fluid is composed of various nutrient hormones that enhance the growth and development of the organism. Normally this fluid flows downward and is burned away by the gastric fire that agitates prana. When complete mastery is gained over jalandhara bandha, the nectar does not flow downward, and the nadis Ida and Pingala, which are lunar and solar currents, respectively, are deadened.

The throat is the location of the fifth center, Vishuddha Chakra, and it binds sixteen supporting organs: toes, ankles, knees, thighs, perineum, reproductive organs, navel, heart, neck, throat/tongue, nose, center of eyebrows, forehead, head, cerebrum, and Sushumna Nadi in the skull. Through regular practice of jalandhara bandha all diseases of the throat are destroyed. The sixteen supporting organs are vitalized, and the soma is recycled into the body. This cerebrospinal fluid is thus channeled to another circuit. These life-giving chemicals are wasted if burned in gastric fire, promoting old age and death. Rechanneling of this fluid through jalandhara bandha removes old age and revitalizes the total organism. It suspends the activity of Ida and Pingala through constriction, causing the prana to flow through Sushumna. This slows down the rate of breath until it becomes motionless. The lifespan is lengthened; diseases are removed; and the practitioner is rejuvenated.

The three bandhas are excellent devices for awakening Kundalini, opening the path of Sushumna, deadening the activity of Ida and Pingala, fusing prana with apana, and perfecting Kundalini Yoga.

The Yogic Mudras

In Kundalini Yoga, mudras are meditation practices in which the eyes are drawn upward so that the top of the iris is not visible. This form of meditation serves greatly in awakening Kundalini. Two mudras, as invariably mentioned in tantric scriptures, are to be practiced for attainment of the ultimate union between Shiva and Shakti:

1. Sambhavi Mudra.

This mudra entails internal meditation on the chakras, and thus it is practiced when the sadhaka begins to concentrate on the chakras. As mentioned above, meditation on the chakras is not concentration on the physical organs or regions, but on subtle centers. To apply such concentration the sadhaka meditates externally on the diagrams of the chakras to establish their images in the mind. These images involve the divine energies present there: the presiding deity of the chakra, the Shakti, the bija (seed) sound, the *vahana* (carrier of the bija), and the *yantra* (diagram) of the chakra. Through inner vision, tantrics (i.e., tantric masters) discovered the forms that are the basis of these diagrams.

The sadhaka who wishes to practice sambhavi mudra for the purpose of arousing Kundalini should first color images of the chakras and meditate on them. After external completion as a preparation for meditation on the chakras, the aspirant then practices internal meditation on the images, which is possible only after they have been retained in the mind. This is done in gradual progression, beginning with the first chakra and continuing through to the second, third, and so on. The center of concentration should not be the gross organs of the body or particular areas, such as the heart. Yogic schools that provide no images of the chakra deities can only suggest that the sadhaka meditate on the heart (Anahata Chakra), the seat of meditation for sambhavi mudra. But knowledge of tantric visualization makes for much more efficacious practice.

When the mind and breath are absorbed by the internal image, and the pupils of the eyes are motionless (even though the eyes are open they do not register external images), sambhavi mudra is achieved.

2. *Khechari Mudra.*

This mudra is practiced by meditating internally on the sixth chakra (Ajna), which is located in the space between Ida and Pingala, at the center of the eyebrows. When prana is directed to flow through Sushumna in the supporting space between the eyebrows, khechari mudra is attained. Prana is made to remain steady in Sushumna with this mudra. The tongue should be turned upward to the roof of the palate; this mudra is also called "swallowing the tongue." One fills the mouth of Sushumna at the rear (root) end with soma nectar flowing from the Soma Chakra. By practicing khechari mudra the sadhaka attains mastery over fluctuations of the mind and achieves unmani avastha, or turiya, the state of unconscious consciousness. The sadhaka practices khechari mudra until *yoga nidra* (yoga sleep) is experienced.

When the external breath is stopped by performing this mudra — for swallowing the tongue blocks the passage of air between the nostrils and the lungs — the breath within the body is suspended. Prana, along with the mind, becomes still in Brahma Randhra. Concentration on Kundalini in this state brings about the final fusion of Kundalini and prana in Brahma Randhra, and the mind and Kundalini unite. Union between Shiva and Shakti takes place — and the highest goal of the true aspirant is thus achieved.

By regular practice of the above techniques, the aspirant will acquire a spiritual attitude. Asanas bring an end to all corporeal activities, and actions are confined to prana and the sense organs. Through kumbhaka, the movement of prana and the sense organs ceases; only mental activity remains. By pratyahara, dharana, dhyana, and samprajnata samadhi, mental activity ceases and action is in buddhi, or the higher mind, alone. By complete destruction of attachment and long and regular practice of samprajnata samadhi, the activities of buddhi also come to an end. The sadhaka achieves a natural state of being: *sahaja avastha*, which is an unchangeable state, the final aim of yoga. The yogi then stays forever in union with Supreme Consciousness.

CHAPTER THREE

Essentials of the Chakras

MULADHARA CHAKRA
(FIRST CHAKRA)

MEANING OF CHAKRA NAME: "Foundation."

LOCATION: Pelvic plexus; region between anus and genitals; the base of the spine; the first three vertebrae.

BIJA (SEED) COLOR: Gold.

BIJA PETAL SOUNDS: VANG, SHANG, KSHANG, SANG.

ASPECTS: Food and shelter.

TATTVA (ELEMENT): Earth.

COLOR OF TATTVA: Yellow.

SHAPE OF TATTVA: Square.

PREDOMINANT SENSE: Smell.

SENSE ORGAN: Nose.

WORK ORGAN: Anus.

VAYU (AIR): Apana Vayu, the air that expells the semen from the male organ; urine for both sexes; and that which pushes the child from the womb during birth.

LOKA (PLANE): Bhu Loka (physical plane).

RULING PLANET: Mars (solar, masculine).

YANTRA FORM: Chrome yellow square with four vermilion petals. The square has great significance with regard to earthly awareness, as it represents the earth itself, the four dimensions, and the four directions. The form of the earth element is linear, and the four points form the four pillars or corners of what is known as the quadrangular earth. Four allows for completion, and earth embodies the elements and conditions for human completion on all levels. This yantra is the seat of the bija sound, and therefore it releases sound in eight directions. This is shown by the eight spears emanating from it. Earth is the densest of

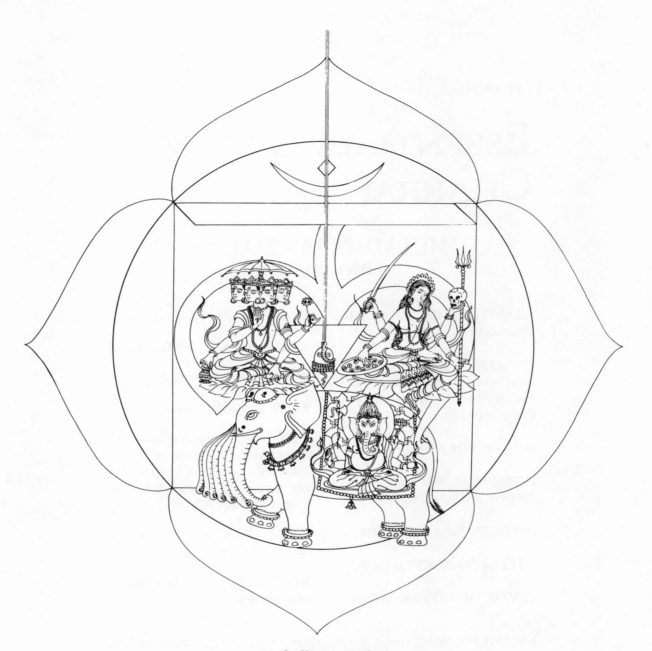

Muladhara Chakra

मूलाधार चक्र

Bija petal sound

वं शं षं सं

all elements, being a mixture of the four other elements of water, fire, air, and akasha.

The Circle with Four Petals: The four lotus petals represent ganglions that are formed at four important nerve endings. The color of the petals is vermilion mixed with a small amount of crimson red.

The Triangle: The seat of the vital life force, Kundalini Shakti, is depicted variously in the form of a coiled serpent, a lingam or a triangle. The Kundalini serpent is coiled three and one-half times around the Svayambhu ("self-born") Lingam. With her mouth open, facing upward, she is connected with the path of Sushumna, the central nerve canal that runs along the spine. The unawakened Kundalini Shakti remains coiled, wrapped around the lingam with her tail in her mouth. Because her mouth faces downward, the flow of energy is downward. As soon as one begins working with the first chakra, this dormant energy raises its head and flows freely into the channel of Sushumna.

The downward-pointing triangle is the yantra of the lingam and Kundalini. It indicates the downward movement and the three main nerves, Ida, Pingala, and Sushumna. The union of these nerves in Muladhara Chakra forms an inverted triangle, which also causes the energy to flow downward. The color of the lingam is smoky gray, sometimes also said to be of the color of a new leaf.

BIJA SOUND: LANG. This sound is produced by putting the lips in a square shape and pushing the tongue in a square shape, against the palate. This bija sound vibrates the palate, the brain, and the top of the cranium.

When properly produced, the bija *LANG* excites the nadis in the first chakra and creates a lock that closes the downward movement of energy. Upward movement starts when the end of the sound *LANG* — that is, *ANG* — vibrates in the upper head. Repeating the sound takes away the insecurities associated with the first chakra and provides the aspirant with financial security, awareness, and inner strength. The bija *LANG* is said to have four "arms." Its vibration helps create a passage inside the Brahma Nadi in order to facilitate the flow of energy.

VEHICLE OF BIJA: The elephant Airavata. Indra, the god of the firmament, rides on his elephant Airavata. The skin of the elephant is soft grey, the color of clouds. The seven trunks of Airavata form a rainbow of seven colors. There are seven aspects of every person which must be recognized and evolved in harmony with natural laws. The seven aspects are:

```
Sound . . . . . . . . . . . . . . . . . . . . . . . . . . . . . . . Ears (sense organ)
Touch . . . . . . . . . . . . . . . . . . . . . . . . . . . . . . .Skin (sense organ)
Sight . . . . . . . . . . . . . . . . . . . . . . . . . . . . . . . Eyes (sense organ)
Taste . . . . . . . . . . . . . . . . . . . . . . . . . . . . . Tongue (work organ)
Smell . . . . . . . . . . . . . . . . . . . . . . . . . . . . . . Nose (sense organ)
Defecation . . . . . . . . . . . . . . . . . . . . . . . . . Anus (work organ)
Sex . . . . . . . . . . . . . . . . . . . . . . . . . . . . . .Genitals (work organ)
```

Similarly, seven *dhatu*s (constituents) make up the physical body:

1. *Raja* — Clay, earth
2. *Rasa* — Fluids
3. *Rakta* — Blood
4. *Mansa* — Flesh, nerve fibers, tissues
5. *Medha* — Fat
6. *Asthi* — Bone
7. *Majjan* — Bone marrow

The seven types of desire (for security, procreation, longevity, sharing, knowledge, self-realization, and union) are seen in the trunks and the seven colors. They are also associated with the seven chakras, the seven notes in an octave, and the seven major planets.

The elephant represents the nature of a life-long search for food for the body, the mind, and the heart. One who has activated the first chakra walks with the steadfast, assured gait of an elephant. He will strive to increase his amount of control with the heaviest weight he can bear. He will do his work with humility, like the manual laborer who carries out continuous orders from others. One who has mastered control over his *indriya*s — the organs of sense and work — is said to become Indra.

DEITY: Bala Brahma (Child Brahma). Brahma, the lord of creation, rules the North and is the presiding deity of the first chakra. He is depicted as a radiant child with four heads and four arms. His skin is the color of wheat. He wears a yellow dhoti (traditional Indian cloth wrapped to cover the lower body) and a green scarf. With four heads, Brahma sees in four directions at once. Each head represents one of the four aspects of human consciousness. These are recognized as the following.

1. *The Physical Self:* Bodily relationship to food, exercise, sleep, and sex. The physical self is manifested through earth, matter, and the mother.
2. *The Rational Self:* The intellect or conditioned logic of an individual's reasoning processes.
3. *The Emotional Self:* The moods and sentiments that shift continually within the person. Loyalties and romance are influenced by the emotional self.

4. *The Intuitive Self:* The inner voice of a person's conscious mind.

In his four arms Brahma holds the following:

- In his upper left hand, a lotus flower, the symbol of purity.
- In his second left hand, the sacred scriptures, containing the knowledge of all creation. Brahma may impart sacred knowledge when he is properly invoked.
- In one right hand, a vase containing nectar. This is amrita, the precious fluid of vital potency.
- The fourth hand is raised in the mudra of granting fearlessness.

Brahma appears during the twilight hours of dusk and sunrise. By envisioning him, one invokes a peaceful stillness in the mind. All fears and insecurities are resolved through Lord Brahma, the ever-watchful creator.

SHAKTI: Dakini. The energy of Dakini Shakti combines the forces of the creator, preserver, and destroyer, symbolized by the trident held in one of her left hands.

In her other left hand she holds a skull, which indicates detachment from fear of death — the basic psychological block of the first chakra.

Her upper right hand holds a sword, with which she removes fear, destroys ignorance, and helps the sadhaka surmount all difficulties.

In her other right hand she holds a shield, which provides the power to shield oneself against problems.

Dakini Shakti has pink skin and wears a sari of either yellow-peach or vermilion color. In some texts she is shown as an angry-looking, fearsome goddess, but for meditation the images of gods and goddesses should be visualized in their pleasant moods. The eyes of Dakini Shakti are brilliant red in color.

RULER: Ganesha. The elephant-headed god, Ganesha, lord of all beginnings, is invoked to bestow protection over all undertakings.

The figure of Ganesha is very attractive yet difficult for the rational mind to accept as an important deity. Worship of Ganesha involves accepting him as remover of obstacles; this subdues the rational mind, or the left hemisphere — which is analytical and critical in nature — and frees the right hemisphere, which is emotional and which is needed for any spiritual venture. Visualization of Ganesha helps in stopping the internal dialogue. One who is put off by the external form cannot admire the internal beauty of Ganesha, but one who penetrates the physical reality can see in Ganesha the union of love and wisdom, Shakti and Shiva.

Ganesha's skin is coral orange. He wears a dhoti of lemon yellow color. A green silk scarf drapes his shoulders. He has four arms to serve him while he acts as the destroyer of obstacles. Ganesha is the son of Shiva and Parvati. He carries the swastika (Sanskrit, *svastika*), the ancient Indian symbol of the union of the four directions, the upward energy of Lord Vishnu, and solar radiation. In his four arms Ganesha holds the following:

- A *ladu*, a fragrant sweet symbolizing sattva, the most refined state of pure consciousness. The ladu also brings health and prosperity to the household.
- A lotus flower, symbolizing the qualities of selfless action and a stainless nature.
- A hatchet, symbolizing control of the "elephant of desires" and the cutting away of the bondage of desires. The hatchet cuts the person away from the false identification of his Self with his physical body.
- The fourth hand of Ganesha is raised in the mudra of granting fearlessness.

EFFECTS OF MEDITATION: Muladhara Chakra represents the manifestation of the individual consciousness into human form, that is, physical birth. Meditation on the tip of the nose induces the beginnings of awareness, freedom from disease, lightness, inspiration, vitality, vigor, stamina, security, an understanding of inner purity, and softness in the voice and in the inner melody.

BEHAVIORAL CHARACTERISTICS IN MULADHARA CHAKRA: If a person with tightened jaws and fists refuses to live in accordance with the natural laws that govern his body, he will create further karma, or worldly entanglement. His sense and work organs will only serve to bring confusion and pain in exchange for temporary gratification. Once a person begins to act in harmony with these natural laws, he will no longer waste energy or pollute his sensory awareness with over-indulgence. Such a person will act wisely and with moderation, exploring his body and mind as vehicles of liberation from the lower realms.

Normally a child from the ages of one to seven years acts out of "first-chakra" motivations. The earth is being grasped as a new experience. The infant must ground himself and establish the laws of his world, learning to regulate his patterns of eating, drinking, and sleeping as the proper behavior necessary for securing his worldly identity. The young child will be self-centered and highly concerned with his own physical survival.

The main problem of the child, or adult, acting from first-chakra motivation is violent behavior based on insecurity. A fearful person may strike out blindly and senselessly, like a cornered animal, due to what is felt to be a loss of basic security.

The person dominated by the Muladhara Chakra generally sleeps between ten and twelve hours nightly, on his stomach. This chakra encompasses the planes of genesis, illusion, anger, greed, delusion, avarice, and sensuality. These aspects of the first chakra are fundamental to human existence. The desire for more experience and information acts as a motivating force, a basic impetus for individual development.

The Muladhara Chakra is the seat of the coiled Kundalini, the vital Shakti, or energy force. The Kundalini serpent is coiled around the Svayambhu Lingam. This foundation chakra is the root of all growth and awareness of the divinity of man.

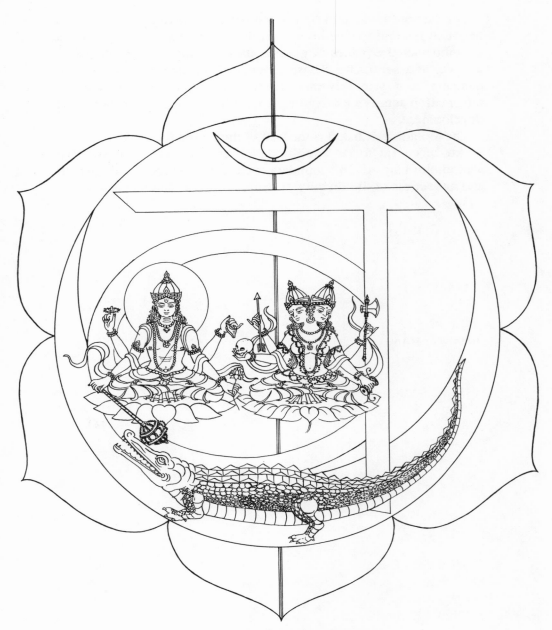

Svadishthana Chakra

स्वाधिष्ठान् चक्र

Bija petal sound

बं भंमं यंरलं

SVADHISTHANA CHAKRA
(SECOND CHAKRA)

MEANING OF CHAKRA NAME: "Dwelling-place of the Self."

LOCATION: Hypogastric plexus; genitals.

BIJA (SEED) COLOR: Gold.

BIJA PETAL SOUNDS: BANG, BHANG, MANG, YANG, RANG, LANG.

ASPECTS: Procreation, family, fantasy. The earth element of Muladhara Chakra dissolves into the water element of Svadhisthana Chakra. Fantasy enters as the person begins interrelating with family and friends. The inspiration to create begins in the second chakra.

TATTVA (ELEMENT): Water.

COLOR OF TATTVA: Light blue.

SHAPE OF TATTVA: Circle.

PREDOMINANT SENSE: Taste.

SENSE ORGAN: Tongue.

WORK ORGAN: Genitals.

VAYU (AIR): Apana Vayu (see description in first chakra).

LOKA (PLANE): Bhuvar Loka Naga Loka, the astral plane.

RULING PLANET: Mercury, (Lunar, feminine)

YANTRA FORM: The Circle with Crescent. The moon-shaped crescent is the yantra of this chakra; it is light blue in color. The form of the water element is circular. The second chakra is dominated by the element of water — the essence of life.

Three-fourths of the earth is covered with water. The ocean tides are governed by the moon. Three-fourths of a person's body weight is water. The moon affects people in the form of "emotional tides." Women have a monthly cycle which is synchronized with the moon cycle. The Svadhishthana Chakra is the center of procreation, which is directly related with the moon.

The vital relationship between water and the moon is shown by the crescent yantra within the white circle of the water chakra. The moon plays a great role in the life of a "second-chakra" person, who goes through many emotional fluctuations during the changing phases of the moon.

The Circle with Six Petals: Outside a white circle are six lotus petals of red (a mixture of vermilion and carmine), the color of mercury oxide. The six petals represent six important nerve endings in the second chakra. As the four petals in the first chakra represent the flow of energy through four sources and through all the four dimensions, the six petals of the second chakra show energy flowing from six dimensions. In the second chakra, the linear awareness of the first chakra becomes circular, with more movement and flow. The white circle symbolizes water, the element of Svadhishthana Chakra.

BIJA SOUND: *VANG.* The concentration should be centered at the second chakra when the bija *VANG* is repeated. Water sounds enhance the power of this bija. When produced in a proper manner, this sound opens any blocks in the lower regions of the body, allowing an unobstructed flow of energy there.

VEHICLE OF BIJA: Crocodile (Sanskrit, *Makara*). Moving with serpentine motion, the crocodile depicts the sensuous nature of the second-chakra person. The crocodile captures its prey through many tricks. It enjoys floating, dives deep beneath the water, and is strong in sexual power. The fat of the crocodile was once used to increase virility in men.

The crocodile's habits of hunting, trickery, floating, and fantasizing are qualities of a second-chakra person. The English saying "to shed crocodile tears" is also known in Indian languages, and refers to a false display of emotion.

DEITY: Vishnu, the lord of preservation. Vishnu represents the power of preservation of the human race; thus he sits in the second chakra, the seat of procreation; he is seated on a pink lotus. His skin is lavender-blue, and he wears a dhoti of golden yellow. A green silk scarf covers his four arms. Vishnu embodies the principles of right living. His nature is lila, or play. He assumes different forms at will and plays different roles. He is the hero of the cosmic drama.

The four arms of Vishnu hold four implements that are essential for the right enjoyment of life:

1. The conch shell contains the sound of ocean waves. The conch of Vishnu represents the pure sound that brings liberation to human beings.
2. The chakra is the ring of light, spinning on the index finger of Vishnu. This chakra is the symbol of dharma. The Dharma

SOMA CHAKRA

SAHASRARA CHAKRA

VISHUDDHA CHAKRA

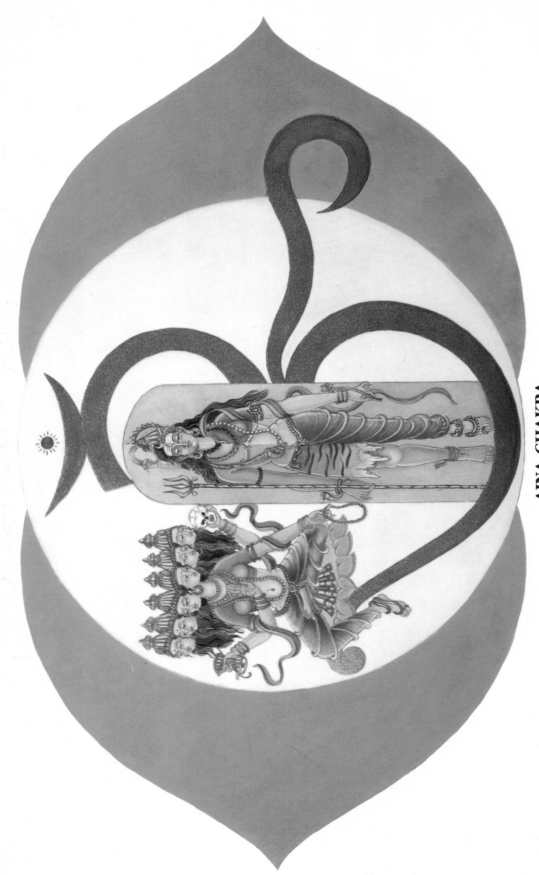

AJNA CHAKRA

MANIPURA CHAKRA

ANAHATA CHAKRA

MULADHARA CHAKRA

SVADISHTHANA CHAKRA

Chakra revolves on its own axis; it cuts through obstacles and destroys disharmony and imbalance. The wheel, the form of the chakra, represents time. Staying true to its revolution, the chakra-wheel creates the cycle of time; whatever is not in conformity with the cosmic rhythm must come to an end.

3. The club is made of metal, an earth element, and it is a tool for maintaining control over the earth. The handle brings control of the earth into the hands of Vishnu. Earthly security in the form of monetary wealth is the first requirement before sensual desires and a sexual life can be fulfilled.

4. A lotus of pale pink color is held in Vishnu's fourth hand. The lotus grows from the mud, yet still remains luminous, radiant, and graceful. The lotus is pure — completely unaffected by its environment. Its flower opens up with the first ray of sunlight, and with the last rays again curls up its petals. Delicate and sweet-smelling, the lotus is soothing to all senses.

SHAKTI: Rakini. Rakini Shakti is two-headed; her skin is pale pink (although according to the *Shat-chakra-nirupan* it is the color of a blue lotus). She wears a red sari, and jewels encircle her neck and four arms. The first inspiration of art and music comes from Rakini Shakti. In her four arms are the following implements:

1. An arrow: Shot from the bow of Kama (the lord of erotic love), this arrow depicts the nature of the second-chakra person as he shoots his arrow to the desired spot; it indicates the impetus for upward movement within this chakra. The arrow of Rakini Shakti is the arrow of feelings and emotions that bring both pleasure and pain as duality arises.

2. A skull: The skull symbolizes the nature of the romantic, who bears his head on his hand, with emotions ruling his behavior.

3. A *damaru* (drum): The drum depicts the power of rhythm and beat in the second chakra.

4. A *purusha* (ax): The ax was the first weapon invented by human kind. With this weapon Rakini Shakti cuts through all obstacles within the second chakra.

The two heads of Rakini Shakti represent the split energy in the second chakra: the effort of the second-chakra person is spent on attaining a balance between the world without and the world within. Expansion of personality begins in this chakra.

In the first chakra the basic motivation was to pursue monetary security; the attention was linear and followed a single direction. In the second chakra the attention is diverted toward desires and fantasies of a sensual nature.

EFFECTS OF MEDITATION: Centering on this chakra enables the mind to reflect the world as the moon reflects the sun. One acquires the ability to use creative and sustaining energy to elevate himself to refined arts and pure relationships with others, having become free of lust, anger, greed, unsettledness, and jealousy.

When Lord Vishnu is visualized, a feeling of peacefulness ensues, as still as a lake. Elevation from the first to the second chakra brings a lunar awareness, reflecting the divine grace of creation and preservation. Vishnu sees all the worlds and preserves the creation of Lord Brahma; he is beneficent with a countenance of the purest nature.

BEHAVIORAL CHARACTERISTICS IN SVADHISHTHANA CHAKRA: Normally a person between the ages of eight and fourteen acts from second-chakra motivation. He will sleep eight to ten hours nightly, in a fetal position. In terms of the elements, the earth is dissolved into water. Instead of standing alone and defensive, as he did in first chakra, the child begins to reach out to his family and friends for physical contact. The imagination increases. Once the need for food and shelter is met, the person is free to visualize any environment or circumstance that he desires. Sensuality enters into relationships as a new awareness of the physical body evolves.

The desire for physical sensations and mental fantasies can be a problem for the person at this level. Gravity causes water to flow downward, and thus, the second chakra can have a downward, whirlpool effect on the psyche, causing a person to be restless and confused. The body and mind have natural limitations which must be respected and understood if the person is to remain healthy and balanced. Eating, sleeping, and sex must be regulated in order to attain a harmonious, peaceful state of body and mind.

A second-chakra person often pretends to be a prince, lord, or hero. He changes roles, maintains high self-esteem, and is chivalrous. Every culture produces an abundance of stories and poems heralding these royal heroes, destroyers of evil.

Svadhishthana Chakra encompasses the astral plane as well as the planes of entertainment, fantasy, nullity, jealousy, mercy, envy, and joy. The astral plane is the space between heaven and earth. Here the earth becomes a jewel and the heavens are within reach. Fantasy may be used to advantage through the crafts and fine arts. Nullity is a state of emptiness and purposelessness. When the world is seen with a negative mind, nothing excites, nothing pleases, all is lost. Envy and jealousy arise from a desire to possess the time or qualities of another. This results in a destructive state of restless anxiety. The plane of joy brings a feeling of deep satisfaction. This joy penetrates the entire consciousness of the person who has evolved beyond the aspects of the second chakra.

MANIPURA CHAKRA
(THIRD CHAKRA)

MEANING OF CHAKRA NAME: "The City of Gems."

LOCATION: Solar plexus; epigastric plexus; navel.

BIJA (SEED) COLOR: Gold.

BIJA PETAL SOUNDS: DANG, DHANG, RLANG (palatal sounds); *TANG, THANG, DANG, DHANG* (dental sounds); *NANG, PANG, PHANG* (labial sounds).

ASPECTS: Vision, form, ego, color.

TATTVA (ELEMENT): Fire.

SHAPE OF TATTVA: Triangle.

PREDOMINANT SENSE: Sight.

SENSE ORGAN: Eyes.

WORK ORGAN: Feet and legs.

VAYU (AIR): Saman Vayu, the vayu that dwells in the upper abdomen, in the area of the navel, helping the digestive system. It carries the blood and chemicals produced in the solar plexus through assimilation. With the help of Saman Vayu the *rasa*, or essence, of food is produced, assimilated, and carried to the entire body.

LOKA (PLANE): Sva Loka (celestial plane).

RULING PLANET: Sun (solar, masculine).

YANTRA FORM: Inverted triangle. The downward-pointing, red triangle is located in a circle surrounded by ten petals. The triangle is the form of the fire element. This chakra is also called the solar plexus, and is dominated by the fire element, which aids in the digestion and absorption of food in order to provide the whole body with the vital energy needed for survival. The triangle is the simplest rigid geometric form: it needs only three sides, and yet is an entity in itself. Visualizations play a great role in the life of a third-chakra person. Fire dominates his consciousness, and his heat can be felt from a distance. The inverted triangle suggests the movement of energy downward.

The Circle with Ten Petals: The petals depict ten important nerve endings, ten sources from which to gain energy. The energy flows in

Manipura Chakra

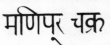

Bija petal sound

डं ढं रां तं यं दं धं नं पं फं

ten dimensions: its pattern is now neither circular nor square; its movement is no longer circular, like that of the second chakra. The color of the petals is blue, like the blue flame of the most luminous part of fire. The ten petals also depict the ten pranas, or vital breaths, as Rudras (primal forms of Shiva). Each petal shows one aspect of Braddha Rudra (Old Shiva).

BIJA SOUND: RANG. This sound is produced by forming a triangular shape with the lips and pushing the tongue against the palate. The main point of concentration when producing this sound is the navel. When repeated in a proper manner, the sound *RANG* increases the digestive power and the powers of assimilation and absorption. The sound also brings longevity, the main object for persons motivated by the third chakra.

The bija *RANG* is always seated in a triangle. The downward triangle of Manipura Chakra has three gates and is crimson red in color. The nature of fire is to move upward, and when the sound *RANG* is properly produced, the fire of Manipura Chakra will move accordingly.

VEHICLE OF BIJA: The ram. The carrier of the bija sound *RANG,* with four radiant feet, is the ram, vehicle of Agni, the fire god. The ram depicts the nature of a third-chakra person: the ram is strong and charges with his head.

The solar plexus is the third chakra, the seat of fire within the body. The third-chakra person is dominated by intellect and fire, which is solar in nature. He lives in a group and moves toward the desired aim without thinking of the consequences — like a ram. Such a man walks with a proud air, as if drunk with vanity. He is very concerned about being fashionable and in step with the times.

DEITY: Braddha Rudra (Old Shiva): Lord of the South, Braddha Rudra represents the power of destruction. All that exists returns to him. He has camphor-blue skin and a silver beard, and sits on a golden tiger skin in his wrathful form, smeared with ashes. The tiger represents manas, the mind.

Third-chakra persons maintain control of others through anger. The countenance of this chakra is of an old, detached person. Identification, recognition, immortality, longevity, and power are the motivations of a third-chakra person. Selfless loyalties to friends and family cease as the person acts only for himself.

SHAKTI: Lakini. In the third chakra Lakini Shakti has three heads; the scope of vision here encompasses three planes — the physical, the astral, and the celestial. Lakini Shakti is armed with both independence and fire. According to the *Shat-chakra-nirupan* she is of dark complexion and the color of her sari is yellow.

In one of her four hands Lakini Shakti holds the thunderbolt, or *vajra* (wand), indicating the electrical energy of fire as well as the physical heat that emanates from within the body. In her second hand, she holds the arrow that is shot from the bow of Kama, the Lord of Sex, in the second chakra. This arrow moves toward the goal, providing the impetus for the upward movement of energy. Her third hand holds fire. With the fourth hand Lakini Shakti forms the mudra (hand gesture) of granting fearlessness.

EFFECTS OF MEDITATION: Meditation on this chakra will bring an understanding of physiology, the internal functioning of the body, and the role of ductless glands as related to human emotions. Concentration on the navel, the center of gravity in the body, brings an end to indigestion, constipation, and all problems of the intestinal region. A long and healthy life is achieved. Egotism is lost, and one achieves the power to create and destroy the world. The fluidity that comes about in the second chakra assumes a form of practicality. Fantasies are brought to practical form, and one develops the power to command and organize. One achieves control over speech and can express ideas very effectively.

BEHAVIORAL CHARACTERISTICS IN MANIPURA CHAKRA: Between the ages of fourteen and twenty-one a person is ruled by Manipura Chakra. The motivation energy of this chakra impells the person to develop his ego, his identity in the world.

A person dominated by the third chakra will strive for personal power and recognition, even to the detriment of family and friends. Such a person will sleep from six to eight hours nightly, on his back.

The plane of Manipura Chakra encompasses karma, charity, atonement for one's errors, good company, bad company, selfless service, sorrow, the plane of dharma, and the celestial plane.

Dharma is the timeless law of nature that interconnects all that exists. By remaining true to one's nature, relationships with others will be more stable and clear. The balance for Manipura Chakra is selfless service, that is, serving without desire for the reward. The practice of charity will clarify one's path of action, or karma. Every person must be aware of his actions in order to achieve a balance in his life. Once this balance is attained, the person may enter the celestial plane of illumination.

ANAHATA CHAKRA
(FOURTH CHAKRA)

MEANING OF CHAKRA NAME: "Unstricken."

LOCATION: Cardiac plexus; the heart.

BIJA (SEED) COLOR: Gold.

BIJA PETAL SOUNDS: KANG, KHANG, GANG, GHANG, YONG, CANG, CHANG, JANG, JHANG, UANG, TANG, THANG.

ASPECTS: Attaining balance between the three chakras above the heart and the three chakras below it.

TATTVA (ELEMENT): Air (formless, without smell or taste).

COLOR OF TATTVA: Colorless; some scriptures indicate smoky grey, and others, smoky green.

SHAPE OF TATTVA: Hexagram.

PREDOMINANT SENSE: Touch.

SENSE ORGAN: Skin.

WORK ORGAN: Hands.

VAYU (AIR): Prana Vayu. Dwelling in the chest region, it is the air that we breathe; and is rich in life-giving negative ions.

LOKA (PLANE): Maha Loka, the plane of balance.

RULING PLANET: Venus (lunar, feminine)

YANTRA FORM: The hexagram. The grey-green hexagram of Anahata Chakra is surrounded by twelve vermilion petals. The six-pointed star symbolizes the air element. Air is prana, the vital life-breath. It aids in the functions of the lungs and the heart, providing fresh oxygen and life force, that is, pranic energy. Air is responsible for movement, and the fourth chakra has movement in all directions.

This yantra is composed of two overlapping, intersecting triangles. One triangle, facing upward, symbolizes Shiva, the male principle. The other triangle, facing downward, symbolizes Shakti, the female principle. A balance is attained when these two forces are joined in harmony.

Anahata Chakra

अनाहत् चक्र

Bija petal sound

कं खं गं घं डं चं छं जं झं ञं टं ठं

The Circle with Twelve Petals: The twelve lotus petals fold outward from the circle, and are of deep red color. They represent the expansion of energy in twelve directions, and the flow of energy through twelve sources. The understanding of the fourth-chakra person is not linear (as in the first chakra), not circular (as in the second), or triangular (as in the third). The fourth chakra expands in all dimensions and directions, as a sixpointed star. The heart chakra is the seat of balance within the body, moving toward a uniform energy flow in both upward and downward directions.

The Circle with Eight Petals. Within Anahata Chakra is an eight-petaled lotus, in the center of which rests the spiritual, or etheric, heart. This heart, known as Ananda Kanda, is toward the right side, whereas the physical heart is on the left. It is in this spiritual heart that one meditates upon his beloved Godhead or on light. These eight petals are connected with different emotions, and when energy flows through them the desire related to that petal is experienced [see diagram].

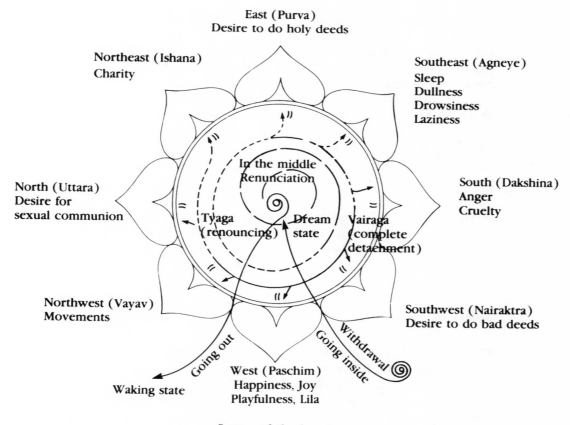

Lotus of the heart

BIJA SOUND: YANG. When the YANG sound is formed, the tongue rests in the air, within the mouth. At this time the concentration should center on the heart. When the bija YANG is produced properly the heart will be vibrated and any blocks in the cardiac region will be opened; when the heart is opened an unobstructed flow of energy becomes free to move upward. This bija gives one control over prana and the breath. It is said to have four arms and to be of radiant gold color.

VEHICLE OF BIJA: *Deer (antelope).* The deer or black antelope is the symbol of the heart itself. The antelope leaps up with joy and is always caught by mirages of reflections.

Very aware, very sensitive, and always full of inspiration, the deer depicts the nature of the fourth-chakra person. The eyes of the deer are symbolic of purity and innocence. The eyes of a fourth-chakra person are equally innocent and pure, as well as magnetic.

The deer is said to die for pure sound. The love of inner sounds, *anahata nada*, is the love of the fourth-chakra person.

DEITY: Ishana Rudra Shiva. Lord of the Northeast, Ishana Shiva is completely detached from the world. With camphor-blue skin, he represents the nature of the fourth-chakra person, which is of perpetual happiness. He wears a tiger skin, symbolic of the tiger of the mind that dwells in the forest of desires.

The nature of Ishana is peaceful and beneficent. He holds the trident in his right hand and a damaru drum in his left. The holy Ganga (Ganges) flowing from his hairlocks is a cooling and purifying stream of self-knowledge: the knowledge that "I am That" (*Aham Brahmasmi*, "I am Brahman"). The snakes coiled around his body are the passions, which he has tamed. He is ever-youthful, as the aged, wrathful aspect of the third chakra is gone.

There is no longer any concern for attachments to worldly pleasures, honors, or humiliations. Desires cease to be a problem, for the energy of the fourth chakra is balanced in all six directions. The person of fourth-chakra awareness lives in harmony with the internal and external worlds.

Shiva in Lingam: The fourth chakra contains a lingam in which Rudra Shiva appears as Sadashiva (*sada*, "eternal"; *shiva*, "benefactor"). He is Shabda Brahma, or the eternal Logos. As such he is Omkara, the combination of the three gunas, sattva, rajas, and tamas, which are represented by the sounds *A, U*, and *M*, respectively, combining to form the sacred syllable *AUM,* or *OM.* He stands with a trident, symbolic of the three gunas. His skin is camphor blue, and he wears a golden tiger skin. The damaru drum that he holds in his other hand maintains the rhythm of the heartbeat.

This *shivalingam* is the second lingam in the body, and is known as Bana (arrow) Lingam, the first being the Svayambhu Lingam of the first chakra, around which the Kundalini serpent is wrapped. The lingam of the fourth chakra is synonymous with conscience. The force of the lingam acts as one's guru. The heart lingam may be the guide, at each step warning or inspiring the aspirant along the path of upward energy movement — as long as one keeps a watch on the heartbeat. An increase or decrease in the rate of the heart serves as a warning that there is an error in one's practice.

This lingam radiates with golden light and is formed from a mass of tissues in the nerve center at the Anahata Chakra. It shines like a jewel in the center of the *chakramala* ("garland of chakras," i.e., the spine), with three chakras above, and three chakras below. Sufis and mystics of other traditions instruct their disciples to visualize a clear light in the heart when beginning the practice of raising the Kundalini force and entering higher states of consciousness. It is here that *anahata nada*, or *shabda brahma* — the unstricken cosmic sound — is produced.

SHAKTI: *Kakini.* The four heads of Kakini Shakti represent the increase of energy in the fourth-chakra plane. Her skin is rose-colored (according to the *Mahanirvana Tantra* it is golden yellow). Her sari is sky-blue and she is seated upon a pink lotus. Kakini Shakti inspires music, poetry, and art. Energy in the fourth chakra is self-generating and self-emanating.

In her four hands Kakini Shakti holds the implements necessary for one to attain balance:

- The sword provides the means to cut through obstacles blocking the upward energy flow.
- The shield protects the aspirant from external wordly conditions.
- The skull indicates detachment from a false identification with the body.
- The trident symbolizes the balance of the three forces of preservation, creation, and destruction.

Kakini Shakti is all-pervading in the fourth chakra. Like air, she penetrates all places and provides energy to the entire body through the emotional frequencies of bhakti (devotion). In the fourth chakra, bhakti is personified as Kundalini Shakti, who becomes an addition and help to Kakini Shakti in directing the upward movement of energy.

Kakini Shakti is in a happy, exalted mood and is meditated upon as a "moon-faced" *(chandramukhi),* four-headed Shakti decorated with ornaments. Her four heads are equally balanced, with energy flowing into the four aspects of the self, that is, the physical self, the rational self, the sensual self, and the emotional self.

Kakini Shakti is responsible for the creation of the poetry and fine art that is based on a refined, visionary level. Mundane art and music, inspired by second-chakra shakti, is unable to elevate the human mind to higher realms of consciousness, but instead will serve only to distract. In contrast, the art inspired by fourth-chakra Kakini Shakti is synchronized with the rhythm of the heart, and thus with the rhythm of the cosmos. The art centered here exists beyond past, present, and future. Fourth-chakra awareness enables the aspirant to transcend the false time-consciousness of lower-chakra persons.

Kundalini Shakti: It is in the heart chakra that Kundalini Shakti appears for the first time as a beautiful goddess. She sits in lotus posture within a triangle. The triangle is pointing upward, showing the tendency of Shakti to move upward and carry the aspirant into the higher planes of existence.

Dressed in a white sari, Kundalini Shakti is serene and centered within herself. She is the virgin mother and is synonymous with *bhakti,* selfless spiritual devotion. No longer is she personified as a destructive serpentine force, as is typified by the first chakra. Kundalini Shakti now becomes a goddess and one may communicate with her, the upward moving energy. She is no longer coiled around the lingam, but sits independently in a yogic posture.

Seated in the lotus posture, Kundalini Shakti embodies anahata nada, the cosmic sound, which is present everywhere and is known as "white noise." This sound begins in the heart as *AUM,* the seed of all sounds. The heart and the breath play vital roles in Anahata Chakra, for the heart is the most important seat of feeling in the body, and when one attains control over his own breath pattern, the heart rate is simultaneously regulated. The person who has realized fourth-chakra consciousness attains refined balance in his body and psyche. The plane of sanctity within this chakra brings the perception of divine grace in all existence.

EFFECTS OF MEDITATION: By evolving through the fourth chakra, one masters language, poetry, and all verbal endeavors, as well as his indriyas, or desires and physical functions. The person becomes master of his own self, gaining wisdom and inner strength. Male and female energy become balanced, and the resolution of the two energies interacting outside the body ceases to be a problem as all relationships become pure. The senses are controlled, and the person flows freely, without hindrance from any external barrier. One centered in the fourth chakra has evolved beyond circumstantial and environmental limitations, to become independent and self-emanating. His life becomes a source of inspiration for others as they find peace and calm in his presence. Divine vision evolves with pure sound in Anahata Chakra, bringing a balance of action and joy. One gains power over vayu, the air element. And because air is formless, the fourth-chakra person can become invisible, travel through space, and enter into the bodies of other persons.

BEHAVIORAL CHARACTERISTICS OF ANAHATA CHAKRA: From twenty-one to twenty-eight years of age one vibrates in Anahata Chakra. One becomes aware of his karma, his life's actions. Bhakti, or faith, is the motivating force as one strives to achieve balance on all levels. This person sleeps from four to six hours nightly, on his left side.

The deer of Anahata Chakra runs swiftly, changing direction often, with an angular path. Similarly, a person in love may have the qualities and tendencies of a deer, such as dreamy eyes, restless wandering, and swift flight. When these come under control all emotional disturbances cease.

Anahata Chakra encompasses *sudharma* (apt or right religion), good tendencies, and the planes of sanctity, balance, and fragrance. Purgatory may be experienced in Anahata Chakra when negative karmas are enacted. Clarity of conscience is the illumination of the pure one who has developed good tendencies and has sanctified his life to Jana Loka, the human plane.

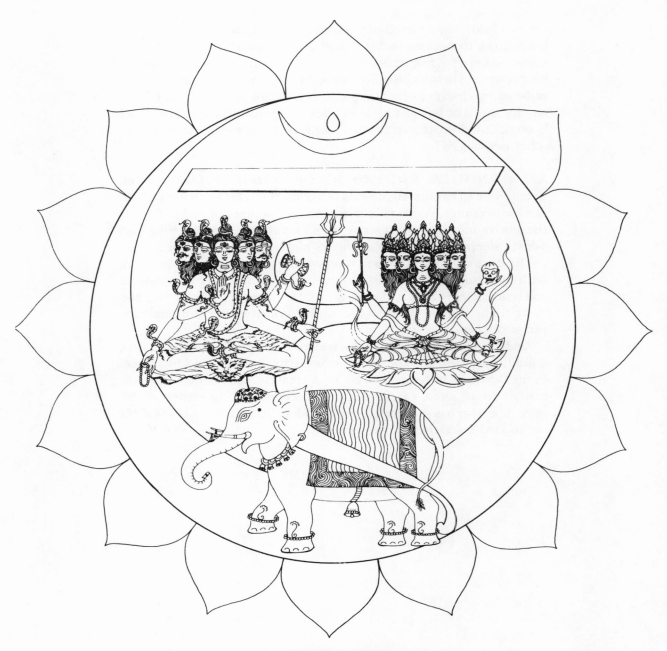

Vishuddha Chakra

विशुद्ध चक्र

Bija petal sound

अं आं इं ईं उं ऊं ऋं ॠं ऌं ॡं एं ऐं ओं औं अं अः

VISHUDDHA CHAKRA
(FIFTH CHAKRA)

MEANING OF CHAKRA NAME: "Pure."

LOCATION: Carotid Plexus; throat.

BIJA (SEED) COLOR: Gold.

BIJA PETAL SOUNDS: *ANG, ĀNG, ING, ĪNG, UNG, ŪNG, RING, RĪNG, LRING, LRĪNG, ENG, AING, ONG, AUNG, ANG, AHANG.*

ASPECTS: Knowledge; the human plane.

TATTVA (ELEMENT): Akasha; sound.

COLOR OF TATTVA: Smoky purple.

SHAPE OF TATTVA: Crescent.

PREDOMINANT SENSE: Hearing.

SENSE ORGAN: Ears.

WORK ORGAN: Mouth (vocal cords).

VAYU (AIR): Udana Vayu, which dwells in the throat region of the head. The tendency of this vayu is to carry air up through the head, aiding in the production of sound.

LOKA (PLANE): Jana Loka (human plane).

RULING PLANET: Jupiter.

YANTRA FORM: The crescent. The yantra of Vishuddha Chakra is a silver crescent within a white circle shining as a full moon surrounded by sixteen petals. The silver crescent is the lunar symbol of nada, pure cosmic sound. The fifth chakra is the seat of sound in the body, located in the throat. The crescent is symbolic of purity, and purification is a vital aspect of Vishuddha Chakra.

The moon in any aspect encompasses psychic energy, clairvoyance, and communication without words; the fifth-chakra person comprehends nonverbal messages, for all energy has been refined. The moon also depicts the presence of the cooling mechanism in the throat. Here all liquids and foods are brought to a temperature suited to the body.

The Circle with Sixteen Petals: The sixteen lotus petals are of lavender grey or smoky purple color. Sixteen completes the cycle whereby one octave ascends and one octave descends around the circle. Here the increase of petals in each chakra comes to an end. Energy flows into the fifth chakra from sixteen dimensions. The expansion of awareness brings the aspirant a vision of akasha. Akasha is of the nature of antimatter. In the fifth chakra all the elements of the lower chakras — earth, water, fire, and air — are refined to their purest essence and dissolve into akasha. Vishuddha Chakra is the top of the *stupa*, or temple, within the body [see diagram].

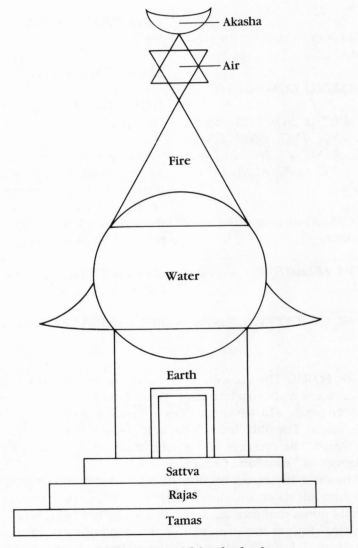

The stupa within the body

BIJA SOUND: HANG. The color of this bija is gold (it is also described as being of radiant white color with four arms). The sound *HANG* is produced by forming an oval with the lips and pushing the air outward from the throat. Concentration is centered in the hollow curve of the lower neck. When this sound is produced properly, it vibrates the brain and causes the cerebrol spinal fluid to flow more fully into the throat, affecting it by bringing sweet and melodious qualities to the voice.

Spoken words come from the fifth chakra, giving voice to the emotions within the heart. The voice of a fifth-chakra person penetrates to the heart of the listener. This pure sound affects the listener by changing the space of his mind and being.

VEHICLE OF BIJA: The elephant Gaja, supreme lord of herbivorous animals. It is of smoky grey color, the color of clouds. Confidence, knowledge of nature and of the environment, and consciousness of sound come in Vishuddha Chakra, as illustrated by the large ears and graceful gait of the elephant. The most primitive of surviving mammals, the elephant carries the entire past knowledge of earth, herbs, and plants. This animal has become the teacher of patience, memory, self-confidence, and the enjoyment of synchronicity with nature.

The single trunk represents sound. The seven trunks of the first-chakra elephant, Airavata, have fallen away. All that remains is pure sound, bringing liberation.

DEITY: Panchavaktra Shiva. Panchavaktra has camphor-blue skin and five heads, representing the spectrum of smell, taste, sight, touch, and sound, as well as the union of all five elements in their purest forms. Beginning with his right, the faces of Shiva symbolize his aspects as follows:

- *Aghora.* He is wide-eyed in his wrath, and resides in the cremation grounds. His face is rounded; his nature is that of akasha.
- *Ishana.* He appears in the shivalingam. He has a rounded face, and his nature is that of water.
- *Mahadeva.* His face is the central one of the five, and is oval in shape. His direction is East; his nature is of the earth.
- *Sada Shiva.* The "eternal Shiva," he has a square-shaped face and thus may expand in all directions; his nature is of the air.
- *Rudra.* Lord of the South, he appears with a triangular face; his nature is of fire.

Panchavaktra has four arms. With a gesture in one of his right hands he bestows fearlessness. With the other right hand, which rests on his knee, he holds a *mala* (rosary) for japa. One left hand raises the damaru drum, which drones continually, manifesting the sound *AUM*. The remaining left hand holds the trident, the staff of Shiva.

Panchavaktra may be visualized in the fifth chakra as the Great Teacher, or Master Guru. All elements have dissolved in one union, and the human plane in all totality is understood. Man realizes his limitations within each element. This awareness of eternal knowledge is grasped when all desires move upward into the sixth chakra. Centering by balancing all of the bodily elements brings a state of blissful nonduality. Through meditation on Panchavaktra, one is elevated and cleansed from all karmas; one dies to the past and is born again into the realization of oneness.

SHAKTI: Shakini. An embodiment of purity, Shakini Shakti has pale rose skin and wears a sky-blue sari with a green bodice. She sits on a pink lotus to the left of her five-headed Lord Shiva. Shakini Shakti is the bestower of all higher knowledge and siddhis (powers). Her four arms hold the following objects:

- A skull, which is a symbol of detachment from the illusory world of sense perceptions.
- An *ankusha*, an elephant staff used to control Gaja. The elephant of intellect can be overly independent, moving in his own intoxication of knowledge.
- The scriptures, representing knowledge of the art of right living without complexes.
- The mala, which acts as a powerful centering device, for the beads are touched with the fingers one by one. When the beads are made of wood or seeds, they absorb and retain the person's own energy. When the beads are cut from crystal, gems, or precious material, they are highly charged with their own electromagnetic energy. The fingertips are directly related to consciousness, and thus engagement of the fingertips is the engagement of consciousness. Working the mala removes nervousness and distractions, and pacifies the internal dialogue.

Memory, ready wit, intuition, and improvisation are all related to Shakini Shakti. The fifth chakra is the center of dreams in the body. Most of the teachings of Shakini Shakti are revealed to her aspirants through dreams.

EFFECTS OF MEDITATION: Meditation on the hollow space in the throat area gives calmness; serenity; purity; a melodious voice; command of speech and of mantras; and the ability to compose poetry, to interpret scriptures, and to understand the hidden message in dreams. It also makes one youthful, radiant *(ojas)*, and a good teacher of spiritual sciences *(brahma-vidya)*.

BEHAVIORAL CHARACTERISTICS IN VISHUDDHA CHAKRA: One who enters Vishuddha Chakra becomes master of his entire self. Here all elements (tattvas) dissolve into pure and self-luminous akasha. Only the tanmatras remain — the subtle frequencies of those elements.

Five work organs are employed in the creation of all karmas: hands, feet, mouth, sex organs, and anus. In addition, there are five koshas (sheaths) of consciousness: the gross, the moving, the sensory, the intellectual, and the feeling. Five is the number of balance, one with two on either side. Being an odd number, five is linked with the solar numbers. The ruling planet of Vishuddha Chakra is Jupiter, which in Sanskrit is called Guru, the one who imparts knowledge.

Earth dissolves into water and remains in the second chakra as the essence of smell. Water evaporates in the fiery third chakra and remains as the essence of taste. The form of fire enters the fourth chakra and remains there as the essence of form and of vision. The air of the fourth chakra enters into akasha and becomes pure sound. Akasha embodies the essence of all five elements; it is without color, smell, taste, touch, or form — free of any gross elements.

Vishuddha Chakra governs between the ages of twenty-eight and thirty-five. The person motivated by the fifth chakra sleeps from four to six hours nightly, changing sides.

The distracting nature of the world, the senses, and the mind ceases to be a problem. Supreme reasoning overcomes the elements and the emotions of the heart. The person will seek only that knowledge which is true, beyond the limitations of time, cultural conditioning, and heredity. The main problem encountered in the fifth chakra is negative intellect, which may occur through the ignorance of using knowledge unwisely.

Vishuddha Chakra encompasses the five planes of jnana (awareness), thus bestowing bliss; prana (the vital force throughout the body), thus affecting a balance of all elements; apana (air that cleanses the body); and vyana (air that regulates blood flow). Jana Loka (the human plane) becomes vital, for here one receives communication of divine wisdom with the sixteen-dimensional, experiential realms, thus bringing about the true birth of man.

One who enters the plane of Vishuddha Chakra follows knowledge, the path that leads to man's true birth into the divine state. All the elements are transmuted into their refined essence, their purest manifestation. When this occurs, being is established in pure consciousness. A person becomes *chitta*, free of the fetters of the world and the master of his total self. The Vishuddha Chakra embodies *chit*, or cosmic consciousness.

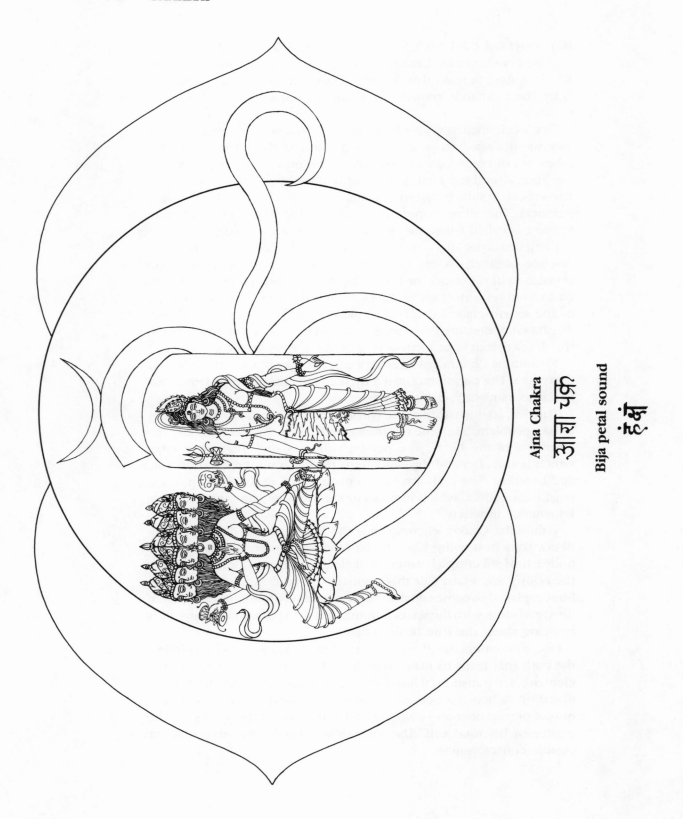

Ajna Chakra

आज्ञा चक्र

Bija petal sound

हंक्ष

AJNA CHAKRA
(SIXTH CHAKRA)

MEANING OF CHAKRA NAME: "Authority, command, unlimited power."

LOCATION: Medula plexus; pineal plexus; point between the eyebrows.

BIJA (SEED) COLOR: Gold.

BIJA PETAL SOUNDS: HANG, KSHANG.

TATTVA (ELEMENT): Maha Tattva, in which all other tattvas are present in their rarified pure essence (tanmatra). According to Samkhya philosophy, Mahat, or Maha Tattva, consists of the three gunas and includes manas, buddhi, ahamkara, and chitta; and from Maha Tattva come the five *mahabhutas* (the five gross elements, i.e., akasha, air, fire, water, and earth). According to Tantra, however, Maha Tattva is the same as Buddhi Tattva, the cause of manas, buddhi, ahamkara, and chitta.

COLOR OF TATTVA: Transparent luminescent bluish or camphor white.

LOKA (PLANE): Tapas Loka, the plane of austerity or penance (*tapasia*).

RULING PLANET: Saturn (solar, male).

YANTRA FORM: White circle with two luminescent petals. These petals are the habernulae of the pineal gland. A lingam appears in the center of the circle.

BIJA SOUND: AUM.

VEHICLE OF BIJA: Nada, also known as Ardhamatra.

DEITY: Ardhanarishvara, the half-male, half-female Shiva-Shakti, symbolic of basic polarity; the right side is male and the left side, female. Ardhanarishvara stands in a lingam known as Itara Lingam. The lingam is shining white, like the color of light.

The male half of Ardhanarishvara has camphor-blue skin. He holds a trident in his right hand, representing the three aspects of consciousness — cognition, conation, and affection.

The female side of Ardhanarishvara is pink. She wears a red sari, and about her neck and arms are wound shining golden ornaments. She holds a pink lotus, a symbol of purity. All duality has ceased. Ardhanarishvara has become the total entity, self-emanating and illustrious.

Shiva has total command over all aspects of the Self in this plane of liberation, or *moksha*. The third eye of Shiva is called *sva-netra*, the organ of clairvoyance. Becoming Sada-Shiva, the eternal one, Shiva is no longer separate from Shakti as a separate male entity. Devata Shiva is the granter of knowledge. This knowledge brings the breath (prana) and the mind under the control of Ardhanarishvara.

SHAKTI: *Hakini.* Hakini Shakti has four arms and six heads. Her skin is pale pink, and her jewelry is golden and shines with gems. Wearing a red sari, she sits on a pink lotus with her left foot raised. She imparts the knowledge of unconditional truth, the awareness of nonduality.

In her hands she holds the following objects:

- Shiva's damaru drum, which maintains a steady drone and leads the aspirant in his way.
- A skull, as symbol of detachment.
- A mala for japa as a centering device.
- Her remaining right hand is posed in the mudra of granting fearlessness.

EFFECTS OF MEDITATION: One who meditates on this chakra eradicates all his sins or impurities and enters the seventh door, beyond Ajna Chakra. This person's aura manifests in such a way as to allow all who come into his presence to become calm and sensitive to the refined sound frequencies of *AUM*; the *AUM* drone generates from the person's body itself. He is now tattvatita — beyond the tattvas. All desires are basically the play of tattva, and thus when one establishes himself in the place between the eyebrows he goes beyond all the kinds of desires that motivate life and impel one to move in many directions. One now becomes one-pointed; he becomes trikaladarsh, knower of past, present, and future. Ida and Pingala are time-bound; up to the fifth chakra the yogi also is time-bound, but as Ida and Pingala end here, the yogi moves into Sushumna, which is kalatita, beyond time. The danger of backsliding ends; there is no spiritual reversal, for as long as he is in his physical body, he is in a constant state of nondual consciousness. He can enter any other body at will. He is able to comprehend the inner meaning of cosmic knowledge and is able to generate scriptures.

The person evolved through Ajna Chakra reveals the divine within and reflects divinity within others. In the fourth chakra he evolves through ananda (beatitude), and in the fifth, through chit (cosmic consciousness). In Ajna Chakra he becomes *sat* (true). There is no observed and no observer. He attains the realization "That I am; I am That," and thus embodies *sat-chit-ananda*, or "being-consciousness-bliss."

The realization in the fifth chakra is *SOHAM* ("That I am;" from *sa*, "That"; *aham*, "I am"). In the sixth chakra these syllables become reversed, thus, *HAMSA*. When the yogi meditates on *atman*, or the Self in the *bindu* (the "dot" representing infinity in the syllable *AUM*), this self becomes known as *HAMSA*, which is also the Sanskrit word for *swan*, the bird that can fly to places unknown to ordinary people. One who dwells in this consciousness is called *Paramhamsa*.

BEHAVIORAL CHARACTERISTICS IN AJNA CHAKRA: The body of the pineal gland protrudes into the third ventricle and is surrounded by cerebrospinal fluid. This clear watery fluid flows from the Soma Chakra (the Moon Chakra), which lies above Ajna. It moves through the hollow spaces (ventricles) in the brain and downward through the spinal cord to the base of the spine. The pineal helps to regulate this flow in a balanced manner. The pineal itself responds very sensitively to light. When a person enters Ajna Chakra, light will form around his head an aura.

Because the yogi brings the breath and the mind under control in this state, he maintains a continual state of samadhi (realized nonduality) during all actions. Whatever he desires comes true, as does the ability to induce visions of the past, present, and future.

The Ida (lunar current), Pingala (solar current), and Sushumna (central neutral current) meet in Ajna Chakra. These three "rivers" meet in Triveni, the main seat of consciousness.

The sixth chakra encompasses the plane of conscience (Viveka), the plane of neutrality (Sarasvati), solar plane (Yamuna), lunar plane (Ganga), plane of austerity (Tapas), plane of violence (Himsa), earthly plane (Prithvi), liquid plane (Jala), and the plane of spiritual devotion (Bhakti).

The third eye is the conscience. The two physical eyes see the past and the present, while the third eye reveals the insight of the future. All experience and ideas serve only to clarify one's perceptions in Ajna Chakra. The plane of neutrality (Sarasvati) appears as a balance between solar and lunar energy within the body. Negative and positive, the components of duality, become equalized in Sarasvati, leaving a state of pure music and neutrality. The solar (Yamuna) and lunar (Ganga) nerve energies interwine up through all chakras and meet with the Sarasvati, becoming one at Ajna Chakra. This brings the sense of oneness and of unity with the cosmic laws that appear in the plane of austerity. The person realizes he is immortal spirit in a temporal body. The lunar liquid plane cools any excessive heat generated by the increased powers, and purifies the conscience. Bhakti Loka, the plane of spiritual devotion, maintains proper balance within the yogi.

In Ajna Chakra the yogi himself becomes a divine manifestation. He embodies all elements in their purest form or essence. All external and internal changes cease to pose a problem. The mind reaches a state of undifferentiated cosmic awareness. All duality ceases.

SOMA CHAKRA

MEANING OF CHAKRA NAME: "Nectar; the moon."

LOCATION: One of the minor chakras within the seventh chakra, Soma is located above the "third eye" in the center of the forehead.

RULING PLANET: Rahu.

YANTRA FORM: Crescent of silver color in a lotus of light-bluish white. Soma Chakra is also known as Amrita Chakra; both *soma* and *amrita* denote "nectar." It is a chakra with a lotus of twelve petals (some scriptures indicate sixteen), in the center of which rests the crescent moon, the source of nectar.

This nectar comes to the moon from Kamadhenu, the wish-fulfilling cow. The nectar is constantly seeping out of the *nirjhara gupha*, or *bhramara gupha* — the hollow space between the twin hemispheres.

Three nadis, Ambika, Lambika, and Talika, along with Kamadhenu, are the four sources of nectar. In its natural course this nectar flows downward, and when it reaches Manipura Chakra it is burned by the solar energy of the solar plexus. By practicing khechari mudra, yogis can block the downward flow of this nectar while enjoying the subtle sounds of nada by meditating on the eight-petaled lotus of Kameshvara Chakra (another minor chakra within the seventh). Here the three nadis Vama, Jyeshtha, and Raudri form the *Ā-KĀ-THĀ* Triangle, which is well known to yogis. Inside this triangle are seated Kameshvari and Kameshvara in eternal union, covered with bluish-white lotus petals.

Ā-KĀ-THĀ Triangle. This form holds a combination of three energies: Brahmi is the energy of creator Brahma; Vaishnavi, of the preserver Vishnu; and Maheshvari, of the destroyer Maheshvara, lord of lords, Shiva himself. These three shaktis flow through three nadis, Vama, Jyeshtha, and Raudri, which form the *Ā-KĀ-THĀ* Triangle. The same triangle made by the same three nadis exists in Muladhara Chakra, where Shiva is in the form of Svayambhu Lingam and Shakti is in the form of a coiled serpent wrapping around that lingam. Vama, Jyeshtha, and Raudri nadis correspond with Brahmi, Vaishnavi, and Maheshvari, respectively. These energies form the three aspects of

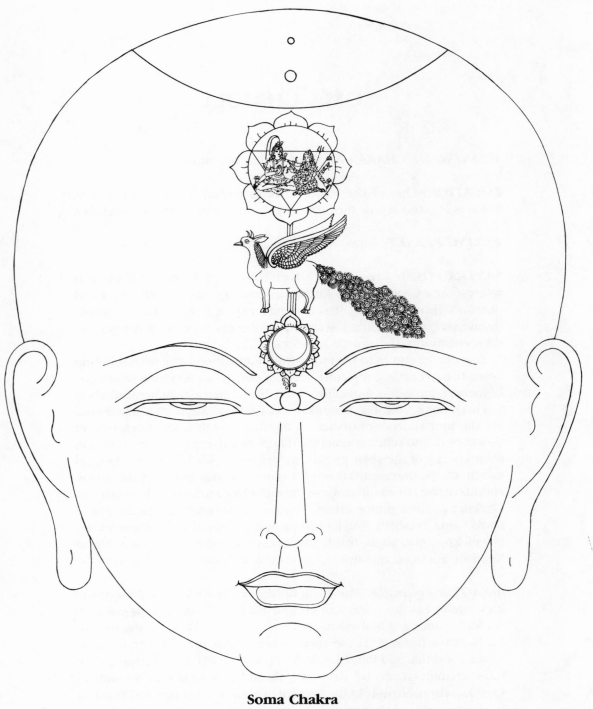

Soma Chakra

सोम चक्र

consciousness: the knowing, the feeling, and the doing, from which emanates the *summmum bonum* of human life — truth, beauty, and goodness. Realization of truth *(satyam)*, beauty *(sundaram),* and goodness *(shivam)* in all forms of expression is the highest aim of life, and incorporating it in one's behavior is the highest state of realization.

DEITIES: Kameshvara and Kameshvari. Kameshvara is Lord Shiva himself. He is the lord of the desire principle (*kama*, "desire"; *ishvara*, "lord"). He is the one who is seated above the famous tantric Ā-KĀ-THĀ Triangle, and whom Devi (Adya, Kundalini, Kula, Tripura Sundari, Tripura, and Kameshvari) is eager to meet; Kameshvari is seated in Muladhara as dormant energy. Through the narrow passage of Brahma Nadi she rushes to meet her lord, Kameshvara, using any of the five movements. Turning the petals of all the lotuses of the different chakras, she reaches the highest one to meet him. Kameshvara is described as the most beautiful of male forms. He is seated like a yogi, but in eternal embrace with his beloved Tripura Sundari, who is Kameshvari, the most beautiful female in the three worlds (*tri*, "three"; *pura*, "planes, worlds"; *sundari*, "beautiful"). Kameshvara is also known as Urdhvareta (*urdhva*, "upward"; *reta*, "streaming, flowing"), for his ability to draw the essence of the seminal fluid upward, through Sushumna; he is lord of the knowledge of the upward movement of energy. Vamachara ("left-handed") Tantra provides a complete description of this process of upward movement, and claims that this is the place where the seed must be brought; here the physical male seed (bindu) unites with the lunar female energy, and the interior and exterior union becomes *tantra* (expanded consciousness), because it is a combination of *bhoga* and yoga, that is, enjoyment and detachment. Kameshvara bestows the power of upward movement and retention of seed; therefore meditation on Kameshvara causes the ego to subside, and the yogi sitting in Soma Chakra enjoys *brahmananda* (bliss of *Brahman*). Kameshvari is now at peace in union with her beloved. She is no more the furious serpent who breathes out fire, as she was when suddenly awakened from her sleep.

EFFECTS OF MEDITATION: One who meditates on this chakra and stops the downward flow of this amrita, or nectar — by performing khechari mudra (*khe*, the ether; *chari*, "moving")—becomes immortal in this physical body. He is able to stop the process of aging, and thus he remains ever young and full of vitality and stamina. He obtains victory over disease, and, decay, and death, and enjoys eternal bliss through the union of Shiva and Shakti — the ultimate goal of kundalini yoga. Khechari mudra enhances the upward flow of energy, and the yogi is able to stay in Gagana Mandala, or Shunya Mandala, "the void,"

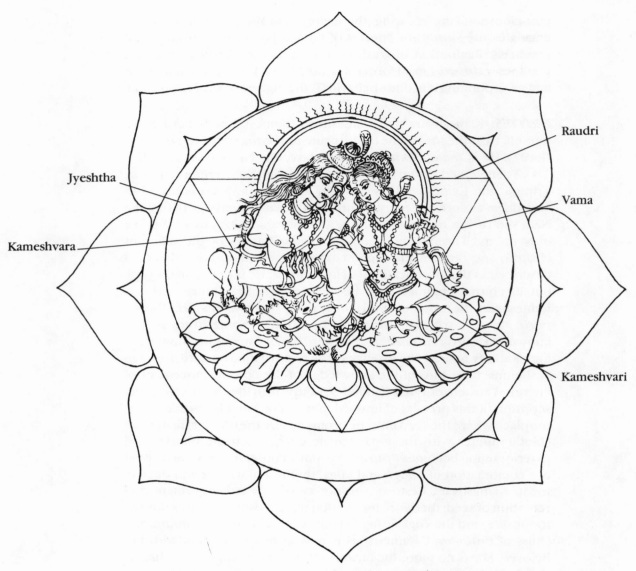

Kameshvara and Kameshvari seated in the Ā-KĀ-THĀ Triangle

ASPECTS OF CONSCIOUSNESS					
Vama	Volition (Iccha)	Feeling	Subtle Sound (Pashyanti)	Creation	Brahmi
Jyeshtha	Knowledge (Jnana)	Knowing	Intermediate Sound (Madhyama)	Preservation	Vaishnavi
Raudri	Action (Kriya)	Doing	Articulated Sound (Vaikhari)	Dissolution	Maheshvari

that is, the hollow space between the twin hemispheres, which is known as the tenth gate of the body. It is located within Sahasrara, the seventh chakra. Soma Chakra is above Ajna Chakra and below Kameshvari Chakra. Soma Chakra is located in alignment with the middle of the forehead and is the seat of soma (the moon), amrita (nectar), and Kamadhenu. The color of Kamadhenu is white; her face is of a crow; her forehead is ahamkara (ego); and her eyes are human, of Brahmic nature. She has the horns of a cow, the neck of a horse, the tail of a peacock, and the wings of a white swan (hamsa).

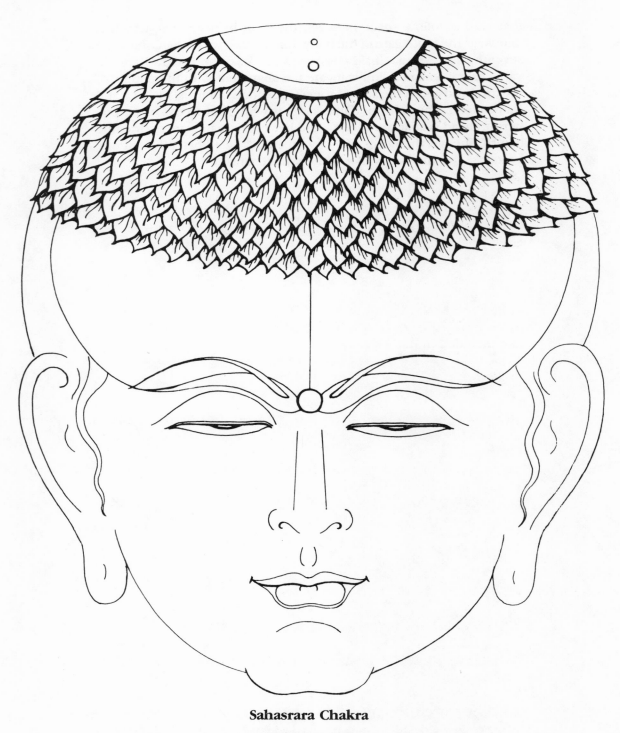

Sahasrara Chakra

सहस्रार चक्र

SAHASRARA CHAKRA
(SEVENTH CHAKRA)

MEANING OF CHAKRA NAME: "Thousand-petaled." Also called Shunya ("empty, void") Chakra and Niralambapuri ("dwelling-place without support") Chakra.

LOCATION: Top of the cranium; cerbral plexus. Soma Chakra and Kameshvara Chakra are included in this location.

BIJA (SEED) COLOR: Gold.

BIJA PETAL SOUNDS: All pure sounds from *AH* to *KSHA*, including all of the vowels and consonants of the Sanskrit language. They are written on the petals in a systematic way.

LOKA (PLANE): Satyam Loka, the plane of truth and reality.

RULING PLANET: Ketu.

YANTRA FORM: Circle as a full moon. In some scriptures the yantra is mentioned as *purna chandra* ("full moon"); in others, as *nirakara* ("formless"). Above the sphere is an umbrella of one thousand lotus petals arranged in the variegated colors of the rainbow.

BIJA SOUND: Visarga (a particular breathing sound in the pronunciation of Sanskrit).

VEHICLE OF BIJA: Bindu, the point above the crescent.

MOVEMENT OF BIJA: As the motion of Bindu.

DEITY: The Guru within.

SHAKTI: Chaitanya. Some scriptures indicate Paramatma, and others, Mahashakti.

PLANES ENCOMPASSED IN SAHASRARA CHAKRA: The following planes are realized by the yogi who has attained seventh-chakra consciousness:

- The plane of radiation (Tejas Loka). *Tejas* is light, fire, or sight in its finest essence. The yogi becomes illuminated like the sun. His aura of light is continually radiant.

- The plane of primal vibrations (Om Kara). *AUM* (or *OM*) is the first sound, continuing infinitely. Here the frequency of *AUM* becomes manifest within the yogi.

- The gaseous plane (Vayu Loka). The yogi obtains supremacy over prana, which becomes so subtle *(Sukshma)* that all of the prana within his body is said to be thumb-sized *(angushtha matra)*; if one were to bring a piece of glass in front of the yogi's nose, no vapors would deposit on it.

- The plane of positive intellect (Subuddhi Loka). All value judgments or dualistic perceptions must be balanced, or negative

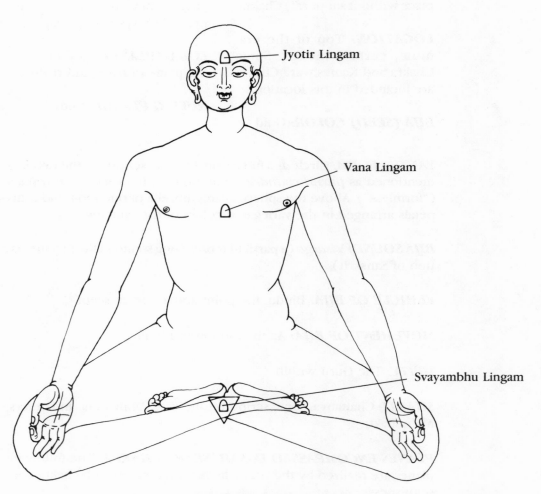

Lingams in the body

intellect *(durbuddhi)*, the negation of the divine, may arise within the mind.

- The plane of happiness (Sukha Loka) arises when a proper balance in body, psyche, and mind is established.
- The plane of laziness (Tamas Loka) may occur when the yogi attains a state of bliss, only to stop all action: when he goes into a state of samadhi, the physical body becomes totally inactive.

EFFECTS OF MEDITATION: Immortality is achieved within Sahasrara Chakra. Before attaining to this chakra the yogi is unable to reach the unconscious conscious state called *asama-prajnata-samadhi*. In this state there is no activity of the mind and no knower, no knowledge, nothing to be known: knowledge, knower, and known all become unified and liberated.

Samadhi is the pure bliss of total inactivity. Up to the sixth chakra the yogi may enter a trance in which activity or form still remains within the consciousness. In Sahasrara Chakra the prana moves upward and reaches the highest point. The mind establishes itself in the pure void of Shunya Mandala, the space between the two hemispheres. At this time all feelings, emotions, and desires, which are the activities of the mind, are dissolved into their primary cause. The union is achieved. The yogi is sat-chit-ananda, truth-being-bliss. He is his own real self, and as long as he stays in his physical body he retains nondual consciousness, enjoying the play of lila without becoming troubled by pleasure and pain, honors and humiliations.

When the Kundalini is raised up to Sahasrara Chakra, the illusion of "individual self" is dissolved. The yogi becomes realized, one with the cosmic principles that govern the entire universe within the body. He obtains all siddhis (powers) up to Soma Chakra, where he encounters Kamadhenu, the wish-fulfilling cow within himself. He is a siddha, but has transcended the desire to manifest those wishes.

According to the shastras, Sahasrara is the seat of the self-luminescent soul, or chitta, the essence of being. Here, chitta is like a screen upon which the reflection of the cosmic Self is seen, and through it the divine is reflected. In the presence of the cosmic Self it is possible for anyone to feel the divine and indeed to realize the divinity within himself.

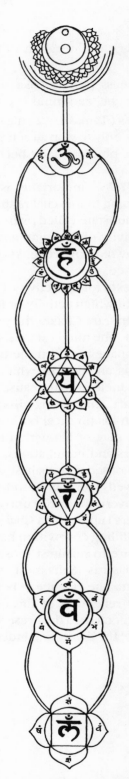

Sounds of the chakras

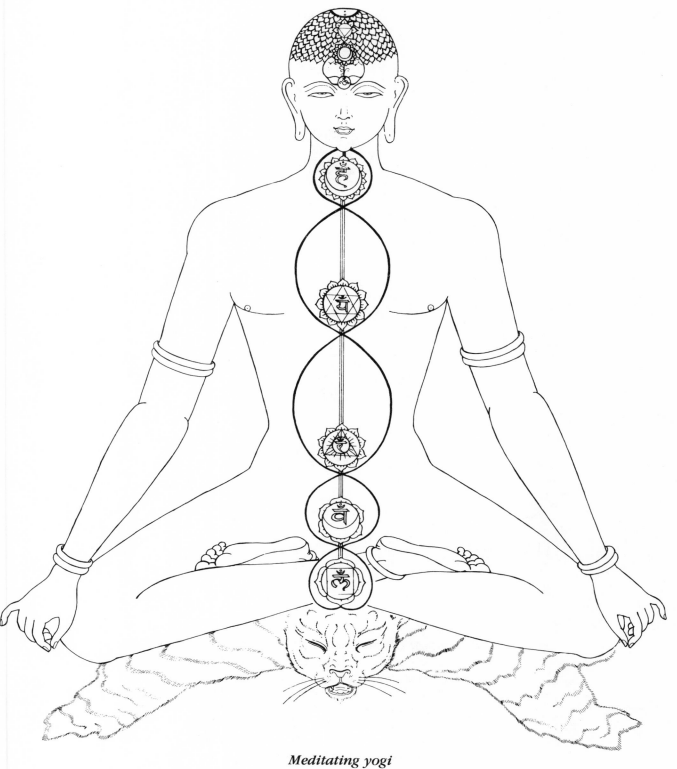

Meditating yogi

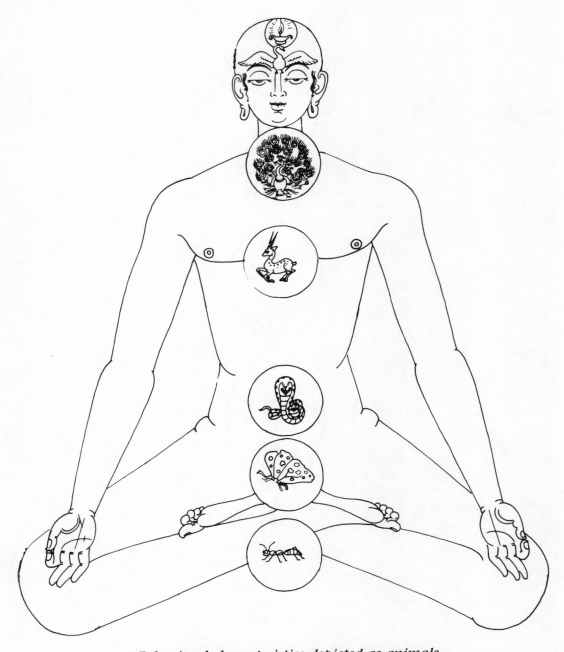

Behavioral characteristics depicted as animals
First chakra — behaves like an ant
Second chakra — behaves like a butterfly
Third chakra — behaves like a cobra
Fourth chakra — behaves like a deer running after a mirage
Fifth chakra — behaves like a peacock
Sixth chakra — behaves like a swan *(hamsa)*
Seventh chakra — pure illumination

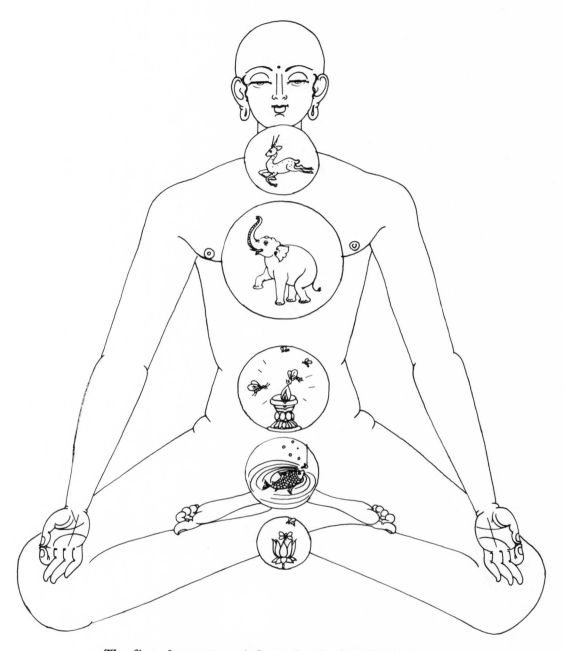

The five elements and the animals that die for them:*

1. Earth — Bumblebee dies for smell
2. Water — Fish dies for taste
3. Fire — Moth dies for sight
4. Air — Elephant dies for touch
5. Akasha — Deer dies for sound

* From the *Vivekachudamani* of Shankaracharya

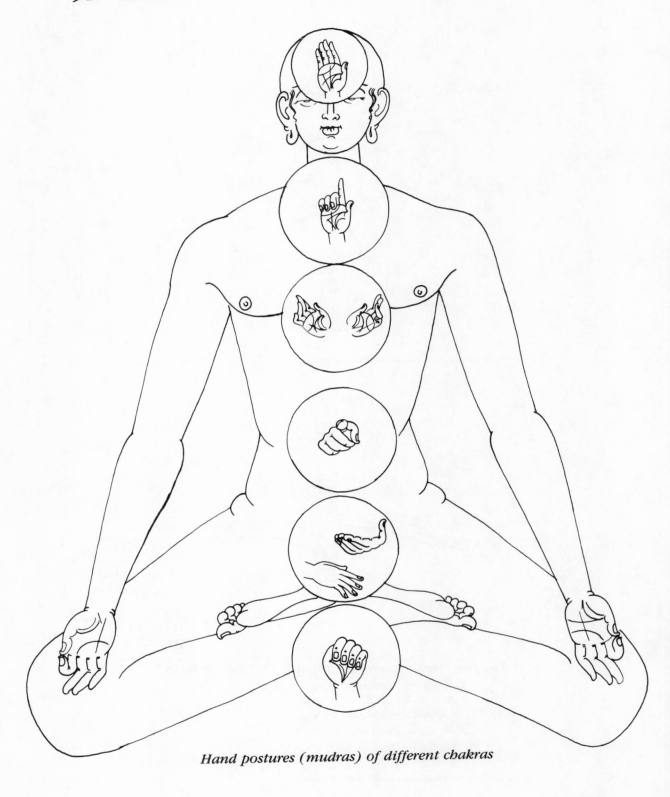

Hand postures (mudras) of different chakras

CHAPTER FOUR

Chakras, Rebirth, and Spirituality

SPIRITUALITY IS THE AWAKENING of divinity in consciousness. It is the summum bonum of consciousness in human incarnation, which frees the consciousness from the mind-body trap. This freedom is obtained by a gradual process of the transformation of sense consciousness (mind).

It is sense consciousness that perceives the world, and that constantly produces uncontrolled thoughts. It desires, senses pleasure and pain, thinks, and wills — and sometimes in its pleasure-seeking aspect commits excesses.

One can be a great thinker, scientist, artist, or educator without the transformation of sense consciousness. But in experiencing only one aspect of one's being — that which is represented by "I"-ness, surrounded by the sensory world — one remains engaged in the gratification of senses, moving aimlessly with lust and greed in the ocean of *samsara*. By transforming the sense consciousness one can achieve freedom from the slavery of mind, lust, greed, uncontrolled thoughts, and internal dialogue. Through the transformation of sense consciousness one can experience the other aspect of one's being, in which the mind is completely detached from the sensory world and does not think, desire, or will. In this aspect the "I"-ness merges into the supreme consciousness and one moves away from the cycle of birth and death.

The "I"-consciousness engages the mind in continual pleasure-seeking patterns, and these experiences of pleasure develop an affection in the mind for sense consciousness. The mind then wanders around and loses its central focus. The "uncentered" mind is then trapped by the objects of the sensory world, which is a play of elements and gunas. An impure mind — or an uncentered mind trapped by desires — leads to bondages, and if the purity of mind is not achieved by constant practice of concentration aided with a mantra, the "I"-consciousness remains — even after leaving the body. It dwells

in different planes (lokas). These planes or lokas are directly connected with the human body through the chakras [see diagram].

The first five chakras are connected with the five elements, and the
lokas connected with those chakras are also connected with those
elements [see diagram]. All mental and physiological activities, all
needs and desires are connected with these five elements. Because
these elements rise and reign in a fixed succession during the flow of
breath through each nostril, the sense consciousness constantly
undergoes a change. The elements — earth, water, fire, air, and
akasha — are agents of the primary inertia principle of consciousness.
They belong to the material field which creates metamatter and
matter, and they constitute a continuum of energy from its most subtle
vibratory level to the most dense.

It is not planet Earth which is called the earth element, but the earth

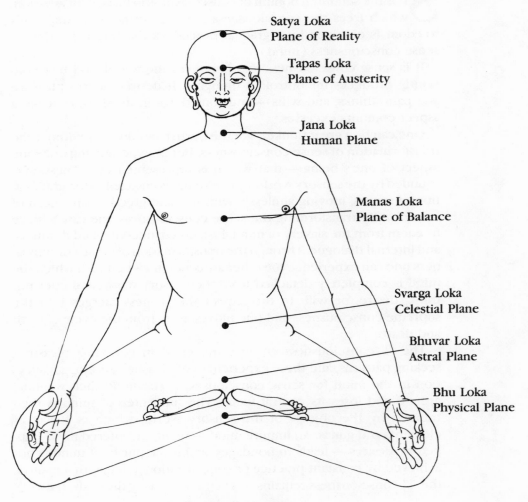

Satya Loka
Plane of Reality

Tapas Loka
Plane of Austerity

Jana Loka
Human Plane

Manas Loka
Plane of Balance

Svarga Loka
Celestial Plane

Bhuvar Loka
Astral Plane

Bhu Loka
Physical Plane

Lokas in the body

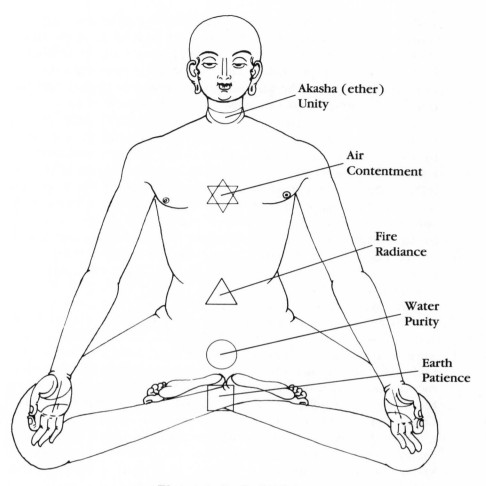

Akasha (ether)
Unity

Air
Contentment

Fire
Radiance

Water
Purity

Earth
Patience

Elements in the body

element dominates in the planet Earth; this planet Earth is known as Bhu Loka. Its seat is Muladhara Chakra. Bones, flesh, skin, nadis, and the hairs in the body consist of the earth element. Patience and greed are its attribute, survival its desire, collecting and saving is the activity which is produced when this element dominates, and its nature is stable. In each breath cycle of sixty minutes (when breath is operating through the right or left nostril) this element dominates for twenty minutes, and one goes through the desires and activities, nature and attributes connected with the Earth element. If the desire for survival remains unfulfilled, one dwells on Bhu Loka after death and takes birth again and again, as a normal human being.

Semen, blood, fat, urine, and mucus (saliva and lymphathic fluids) in the body belong to the water element. Purity and attachment are its attributes, meeting people (family) its desire, peaceful jobs are the activity of this element, and it is cool in nature; in each breath cycle of sixty minutes this element dominates for sixteen minutes. If the desires of the second chakra are not satisfied one dwells in Bhuvar Loka (astral plane) after death. After the period of dwelling in Bhuvar Loka comes to an end, the person takes birth again on earth to fulfil the desire — as, for example, an artist, musician, dancer, or poet.

Hunger, thirst, sleep, lethargy, and lustre (*ojas*, radiance) are related to the fire element. Anger is its attribute. By nature the one dominated by fire is hot-headed and is dominated by the desire for achievement. Hard labor is the activity of this element. In each breath cycle of sixty minutes this element dominates for twelve minutes. If the desires for achievement — name, fame, immortality, power, etc., which are related with the third chakra — are not satisfied after death, one dwells in the Svarga Loka (celestial plane) by virtue of the good karmas (works) done on earth. After the period of dwelling in Svarga Loka comes to an end one again takes birth on earth, as a king or administrator of some kind.

Running, hunting, using strength, shrinking (contraction), and growth of the body (expansion) are related to the air element. It creates restlessness, activity, movement, and a desire to do something. Air is responsible for all kinds of movements inside and outside the body, whether circulation of the blood, or the fluids, lymph, or neuro-motor signals in the nervous system. Air is prana, energy in the form of life force, which makes one a living and conscious being; in each breath cycle of sixty minutes the air element dominates for eight minutes. If desires of the fourth chakra are not satisfied in one's life, then after death one dwells in Maha Loka by the virtue of one's good karmas of love, sharing, devotion, selfless service, and compassion done on earth. After Maha Loka (plane of balance) one again takes birth on earth, as a reformer, a saintly person, a devotee, a healer, or a spiritual artist of some kind.

Love, enmity, shyness, fear, and attachment are related to the akasha element. Its attribute is ego or "I"-ness, its nature is void, its desire is solitude, its activity is thoughts and ideas. In each breath cycle of sixty minutes this element dominates for four minutes. In its final ten breaths Sushumna operates, and then the nostril changes to the other side. If the desires of the fifth chakra are not fulfilled in this lifetime, then after death one dwells in Jana Loka (human plane) for a period of time earned through good karmas during life on Earth. After Jana Loka the person again takes birth on planet Earth, as a teacher, a sage, or an interpretor of holy scriptures.

When one goes beyond the elements through the practice of yoga of any kind one reaches Tapas Loka and performs tapas (austerity), purifies the mind, and through the transformation of sense consciousness experiences the other aspect of one's being. One becomes non-acquisitive, clean, content, and a neutral observer of life and its psychodrama. Mercy, honesty, forgiveness, and firmness enrich this person's life and he or she experiences a splendrous, divine inner force that removes the burden of body consciousness. He achieves full control over his breath and mind, yet he can take birth if the task of self-realization — which is merging of "I"-ness into supreme consciousness — has not been accomplished. Then he is born as an ascetic, a yogi, an avatara, a bodhisattva, or a prophet. He has gone beyond the elements but still must go beyond the gunas, and this is only possible through the practice of awakening Kundalini.

Kundalini is the spiritual energy which lies dormant in Muladhara Chakra. The body can function with its chemical, mechanical, and electrical energy, and the mind as sense consciousness, without awakening spiritual energy, but the objective images will always bind the consciousness, and "I"-ness will bring one back to the cycle of life and death. All beings are subject to the law of karma. Good karmas lead to good lokas and bad karmas to underworlds, or *narakas*. These are connected with the seven chakras *below* the Muladhara, which have not been discussed in this book. Kundalini is the energy that supports life and consciousness while remaining coiled, but when it is awakened it brings spiritualized superconsciousness. The sense-mind is transformed into pure mind, which is absorbed by the stream of consciousness flowing in the form of Kundalini Shakti. The mind goes beyond all contraries and realizes the pure being, the changeless, and the only truth in the form of nirvikalpa samadhi.

After reaching the Sahasrara Chakra and uniting with her counterpart, SHIVA, Kundalini remains in union for some time; she then descends to Muladhara and recoils. During this process of descent, the powers of the chakras and of the deities residing in them are restored. One now lives in an extended state of consciousness. He lives in the body and exhausts his karmas, but as a changed person — and achieves nirvana when he leaves the body.

The body thus purified by yoga does not decay or decompose easily, like the body of the one who is clinging to the material world and the desires for worldly pleasure.

Extracts from Hindu Scriptures on the Various Stages of Yoga

YOGA

The state of real absorption of consciousness, which is beyond all knowledge, is yoga.

(Akshyopanishad 2.3)

Yoga brings a state of deep concentration.

(Shardatilaka 25.1)

A yogi attains yoga only in superconcentration.

(Rudrayamalatantra, Part 2, 27.43)

By developing equanimity of the mind, getting beyond all contraries of the world and of the body-consciousness, one is able to realize the one which is pure being, changeless, beyond mind and speech, and the only truth in the transitory world of mind-power-matter. That brahman is realized directly in yoga in the form of nirvikalpa samadhi.

(Mahanirvanatantra 3, 7–8)

Yoga is the control of the *vritti*s (mental modifications).

(Shandilyopanishad 1.7.24)

ASANA (Posture)

The body should be trained to be in a state of motionlessness for a prolonged time without discomfort or pain.

(Nadabindu Upanishad 3.3.1)

In samadhi all senses cease to function and the body remains motionless like a piece of wood.

(Nadabindu Upanishad 3.3.2)

The three worlds are conquered by him who has mastered posture.

(Trishikhibrahmanopanishad, mantra section 52)

For purification of the body and for attaining success in yoga, posture is absolutely necessary.

(Rudrayamalatantra Part 2.24, 38–39)

Posture helps to make the mind calm.

(Tantrarajatantra 27, 59)

By the practice of posture the body becomes disease-free, firm, and efficient.

(Grahayamala chapter 2, p. 85)

Physical movements (mudras) are not helpful in themselves, nor does concentration alone bring success. One who combines concentration with physical control achieves success and becomes immortal.

(Ishopanishad 9 and 11)

The yogi should use his body as the lower piece of wood and pranava (AUM) the upper piece of wood, and strike them against each other until the fire of realization kindles and he realizes the supreme being.

(Shvetashvataropanishad 1.14)

When the yogi attains a body purified by yoga-fire he becomes free from decay and disease, his youth is prolonged, and he lives long. He then experiences superior smell, taste, sight, touch, and sound.

(Shvetashvataropanishad 2.12)

Asana when mastered can destroy all diseases and can even assimilate poisons. If it is not possible to master all asanas master only one and be comfortable with it.

(Shadilyopanishad 1.3.12–13)

PRANAYAMA (Breath Control)

There are two causes that make the mind wander around: (1) Vasanas — desires that are produced by the latent impressions of feelings, and (2) breathing.

If one is controlled the other automatically gets controlled. Of these two, breath should be controlled first.

(*Yogakundalyupanishad* 1.1–2)

The breathing process creates images in the mind. When breath becomes calm mind also becomes calm.

(*Yogakundalyupanishad* 89)

The control of breath causes both physical and mental development.

(*Varahaupanishad* 5.46–49)

When the nadis are purified by nadishodhana pranayama the prana enters sushumna with a force, and the mind becomes calm.

(*Shandilyopanishad* 1.7.9.10)

Assume first a yoga posture (asana);
keep the body erect, let the eyes be fixed and jaws relaxed
so that the upper teeth do not touch the lower teeth.
Turn back the tongue.
Use the chin lock (*jallunderbandha*)
and your right hand to breathe through any nostril at will;
keep the body motionless and mind at ease.
Then practice Pranayama.

(*Trishikhibrahmanopanishad*, mantra section 92–94)

First exhale the air from the lungs through the right nostril by closing the left nostril with the fingers of the right hand. Then inhale through the left nostril counting 16 — then suspend the breath counting 64 — then exhale through the right nostril, counting 32.

(*Trishikhibrahmanopanishad*, mantra section 95–98)

Ten forms of prana are controlled by Pranayama: (1) Prana, (2) Apana, (3) Samana, (4) Vyana, (5) Udana, (6) Kurma, (7) Krikila, (8) Naga, (9) Dhananjaya, and (10) Deva Dutta.

(*Mundamalatantra*, chapter 2, p. 3.)

By pranayama the throbbing of the prana is controlled and the mind becomes calm.

(*Gandharvatantra*)

By pranayama the internal impurities are removed. It is the best yoga practice. Without its help liberation is not possible.

(*Gandharvatantra*, chapter 10, p. 47)

By pranayama the mind and the senses are purified.

(*Kularnavatantra*, chapter 15, p. 75)

One who is healthy, eats moderately, and can control the breath becomes a yogi.... He who is clean and practices sexual control is able to control breath. Regular practice is absolutely necessary. Yoga is not possible without pranayama.

(*Rudrayamalatantra*, Part 2.17.40–43)

In the first stage of pranayama perspiration occurs, in the second stage the body shakes, in the highest or third stage the body levitates. Pranayama should be practiced regularly until the third stage is reached.

(*Shardatilaka* 25.21–22)

When breath control is perfected, the body becomes light, countenance becomes cheerful, eyes become bright, digestive power increases, and it brings internal purification and joy.

(*Grahayamalatantra*, chapter 13, p. 102)

PRATYAHARA (Withdrawal)

The senses and the work organs should be withdrawn into the manas (sense-mind) and the manas should be absorbed into the jnanathman (consciousness).

(*Kathopanishad* 1.3.13)

The senses should be controlled by will inside the *hrit* (eight-petalled lotus inside the heart chakra, i.e., Ananda Kanda or spiritual heart).

(*Shvetashvataropanishad* 2.8)

By the concentrated mind the senses should be controlled at their root — in the chakras.

(*Trishikhibrahmanopanishad*, mantra section 115)

The mind should be withdrawn by concentrating on the eighteen adharas (vital points), one after another, in the following order, while practicing kumbhaka (breath suspension): (1) big toe, (2) ankle, (3) calf, (4) knee, (5) thigh, (6) anus, (7) genitals, (8) abdominal region, (9) navel, (10) heart, (11) wrist, (12) elbow, (13) neck, (14) tip of the nose, (15) eyes, (16) root of the palate, (17) space between the eyebrows, and (18) forehead. The withdrawal of the senses (*indriya aharona*) from the object by applying the power of control (will) is called pratyahara.

(*Darshanopanishad* 7.1–2)

Breath should be suspended with concentration applied to the following points in succession: (1) roots of the teeth, (2) neck, (3) chest, (4) navel, (5) base of the spine, i.e. the region of Kundalini, (6) Muladhara (coccygeal region), (7) hip, (8) thigh, (9) knee, (10) leg, and (11) big toe. This is called pratyahara by the ancient yogis.

(*Darshanopanishad* 7.5–9)

The control of mind in respect to sensory objects is pratyahara.

(*Mandalabrahmanopanishad* 1.7)

The withdrawal of the senses from their respective objects towards which they are naturally attracted is called pratyahara.

(*Yogalattusopanishad* 68.69)

Pratyahara is withdrawal of the senses from their objects, regarding sensory images as God, abandoning the fruits of actions, turning away from all objects, and holding attention in concentration on the eighteen adharas in the following succession in ascending and descending order: (1) foot, (2) big toe, (3) ankle, (4) leg, (5) knee, (6) thigh, (7) anus, (8) genitals, (9) navel, (10) heart, (11) neck, (12) larynx, (13) palate, (14) nostrils, (15) eyes, (16) the space between the eyebrows, (17) forehead, and (18) head.

(Shandilyopanishad 8.1–2)

Fluctuations in mind are caused by desires; when desires are controlled by pratyahara, the mind becomes still and concentrates on God.

(Rudrayamalatantra, Part 2, 24.137)

The mind connected with senses and their objects is irresistible, firm, difficult to control, and unwilling to obey; the withdrawal of it by the power of will is called pratyahara. By practice of Pratyahara the yogi becomes calm and is able to concentrate deeply. This leads him to yoga.

(Rudrayamalatantra, Part 2, 27.28–30)

In kumbhaka (suspension of breath) the mind should be concentrated; beginning from Muladhara to other chakras step by step — this is called pratyahara.

(Tantrarajatantra 27, 70)

DHARANA (Concentration)

Dharana is holding the divine spirit in consciousness during concentration.

(*Amritnadopanishad* 15)

The withdrawal of consciousness from the perceptive field and holding it in the superconscious field is dharana.

(*Mandalabrahmanopanishad* 1.1.8)

A practitioner of yoga after practicing yama, niyama, *asana*, and pranayama should hold his mind on the five forms of elements in their respective centers within the body. This is called dharana.

(*Trishikhibrahmanopanishad*, mantra section 133–134)

Dharana is of three kinds:

1. holding concentration of the divine aspect of the self

2. holding concentration on akasha (void) in the hrit center (the spiritual heart inside the Anahata Chakra with an eight-petalled lotus)

3. holding concentration on the five divine forms: (1) Brahma, (2) Vishnu, (3) Bridhrudra, (4) Ishan Siva, and (5) Panchavaktra

(*Shandilyopanishad* 1.9.1)

Whatever is seen with the eyes, heard with the ears, smelled with the nose, tasted with the tongue, and touched by the skin should be regarded as divine being.
In this manner the object of the senses should be transformed into divine being and held in consciousness.

(*Yogatattvopanishad* 69–72)

Concentration on big toe, ankle, knee, scrotum, genitals, navel, heart, neck, throat, uvula, nose, space between the eyebrows, breast, and head in kumbhaka (breath suspension) is called dharana.

(*Gandharvatantra*, chapter 5, p. 25)

The holding in consciousness of certain vital points while holding the breath is called dharana.

(*Prapanchasaratantra* 19, 21–22)

Concentration on the six subtle centers and Kundalini (the coiled power) is termed dharana.

(Rudrayamalatantra, Part 2, 27, 34–35)

Concentrating on the universal form of God, realized by concentration on mantra, and then concentrating on God without form is dhyana.

(Darshanopanishad 9.1–2–3–5)

Concentration on the whole divine form is dhyana (meditation) while concentration only on one point at a time is dharana.

(Bhutashuddhitantra, chapter 9, p. 8)

DHYANA (Meditation)

Eyes cannot see the supreme being nor can words express it — nor can it be reached by other senses and cognitive faculties. The supreme being is only revealed in dhyana. Dhyana (true meditation) is only possible when consciousness is spiritualized by purity of knowledge of the self.

(Mundakopanishad 8.1.8)

Dhyana is concentration on the divine being, who is quiescent, luminous, pure, and blissful in the hrit center (spiritual heart).

(Kaivalyopanishad 5)

Concentration on the universal form of God, realized by concentration on mantra, and then concentrating on God without form is dhyana.

(Darshanopanishad 9.1–2–3–5)

When concentration reaches the phase of nondual consciousness (seeing the supreme being abiding in each and every particle), that is dhyana.

(Mandalabrahmanopanishad 1.1.9)

Dhyana is of two types: (1) Saguna dhyana, meditation on God with form and attributes, and (2) Nirguna dhyana, meditation on God without form and attributes.

Doing breath suspension and meditation on the deity is saguna dhyana, and meditation on the supreme being without form is nirguna dhyana. Nirguna dhyana leads to samadhi.

(Yogatattvopanishad 105)

Dhyana is to hold the form of the deity in the consciousness without interruption.

(Prapanchasaratantra 19.22–23)

Dhyana is concentration on the form of the deity of the mantra.

(Kularnavatantra, chapter 17, p. 83)

SAMADHI

The state in which consciousness is in concentration and is illuminated by the divine light — without any desire — that superconscious state is called samadhi.

(Annapurnopanishad 1.48)

By sensory control, control of desires, concentration, and ascesis a yogi will be in samadhi. In samadhi all love is directed toward the supreme being; one is fully attached and absorbed in Him and experiences all bliss in Him. From samadhi, knowledge contained in the word-form (pranava) is revealed to the yogi.

(Nrisinghalapinyopanishad 2.6.4)

The continous flow of consciousness in the form of the brahman, the supreme being in which the I-ness has been dissolved, is called *samprajnata samadhi*. It is attained by prolonged practice of dhyana.

(Muktikopanishad 2.53)

The mind operating at the sensory level is the root cause of all worldly knowledge. If the mind is dissolved, there will be no worldly knowledge. Therefore keep the consciousness fixed on the supreme being in deepest concentration.

(Adhyatmopanishad 26)

Samadhi is that state in which consciousness is only in the nature of the object concentrated on and is still, like the flame of a lamp in a windless place, and from which the feeling of the action of concentration and I-ness ("I am concentrating") has gradually disappeared.

(Adhyatmopanishad 35)

That state in which the mind is devoid of restlessness, I-ness, pleasure, pains, and in which consciousness is absolutely motionless like a rock, in deepest concentration, is samadhi. The state in which there is tranquility is samadhi.

(Annapurnopanishad 1.49–50)

That state of consciousness in which there are no objects, no passions, no aversions, but there is supreme happiness and superior power, is samadhi.

(Mahopanishad 4.62)

When consciousness reaches a state in which it becomes uniform (nondual) it is samadhi.

(*Amritanadopanishad* 16)

Samadhi is that in which the consciousness in deepest concentration and awareness becomes united with supreme consciousness.

(*Darshanopanishad* 10.1)

Samadhi is that in which the I-consciousness *(ekata)* merges in supreme consciousness.

(*Gandharvatantra*, chapter 5, p. 26)

As a crystal of salt thrown into water dissolves in water and becomes one with water so the state in which unity in "I" consciousness and supreme consciousness is achieved is called samadhi.

(*Saubhagyalakshmi Upanishad* 2.14)

Samadhi is that state in which "I" consciousness and supreme consciousness become one. It is without duality and full of bliss, and therein remains only supreme consciousness.

(*Shandilyopanishad* 1.11.1)

When concentrative consciousness is lost it is samadhi.

(*Mandalabrahmanopanishad* 1.1.10)

When the uniform concentrative consciousness is dissolved by the most intensified concentration. there remains only the being of supreme consciousness.

(*Annapurnopanishad* 1.23)

When the deepest concentration on the supreme brahman also disappears by itself within, there arises nirvikalpa samadhi — in which all latent impressions of feelings are eliminated.

(*Annapurnopanishad* 4.62)

INDEX

Numbers in italics indicate illustrations

113

SOUNDS OF TANTRA

Mantra Meditation Techniques from **Tools for Tantra**

A companion to his book Tools for Tantra, Sounds of Tantra provides exact pronunciation of mantras, or words of power. Meditate on the colorful geometric paintings of yantras in the book while listening to the tape, combining visual and auditory elements, or simply listen to the tapes as background for meditation.

ISBN 0-89281-016-5
$15.95 Boxed set of two 60-minute audiocassettes

SOUNDS OF THE CHAKRAS

A companion to Chakras: Energy Centers of Transformation, this audiocassette provides the accurate sounds for meditation on each of the chakras. Johari goes through the entire intonation cycle that is to be practiced with chakra meditation in a way that the student can follow with ease.

ISBN 0-89281-307-5
$9.95 one 40-minute audiocassette

ATTUNEMENTS FOR DAWN AND DUSK

Drawing upon ancient Indian ragas, or musical compositions, Harish Johari creates meditation music especially for the early morning and evening hours, inspired by the sounds of nature, which vary depending upon the hour of the day. *Flute for Dawn, Tambura for Morning Meditation, Flute and Bird for Dusk* are just a few of the selections included.

ISBN 0-89281-370-9
$15.95 Boxed set of two 60-minute audiocassettes

LEELA: THE GAME OF SELF-KNOWLEDGE

The origin of Herman Hesse's Glass Bead Game and the precursor to the popular game "chutes and ladders,"*Leela* is the 2,000-year-old Hindu game of life, in which players' progress is directed by the fall of a die. Repeated play will reveal past karmas, concern, and the patterns governing your life. *Leela* is both entertaining and enlightening, and represents the spiritual journey toward liberation.

"Unlocks the knowledge of the Vedas, Shrutis, Smiritis and Puranas. A seriously fun way to discover self." **The Book Reader**

ISBN 0-89281-419-5
$24.95 boxed set, book, game board, and die

CHANTS TO THE SUN AND MOON

Japa for Energizing the Planets Within

Japa—the repetition of a mantra—is an age-old Hindu technique for drawing down a planet's positive energy. On this recording, Harish Johari chants the preferred number of repetitions of the mantras traditionally associated with the sun and moon. During meditation, the practitioner not only hears the matras intoned by an expert, but is freed from the distraction of counting.

ISBN 0-89281-563-9
$9.95 one 60-minute audiocassette